ASK,
Don't Tell

∾⟡∾

POWERFUL
QUESTIONING
IN THE CLASSROOM

ASK,
Don't Tell

POWERFUL
QUESTIONING
IN THE CLASSROOM

ANGELA PEERY
POLLY PATRICK
DEB MOORE

LEAD+
LEARN
PRESS

ENGLEWOOD, COLORADO

The Leadership and Learning Center
317 Inverness Way South, Suite 150
Englewood, Colorado 80112
Phone 1.866.399.6019 | Fax 303.504.9417
www.leadandlearn.com

Published by Lead + Learn Press, a division of Houghton Mifflin Harcourt.

Library of Congress Cataloging-in-Publication Data

Peery, Angela B., 1964- author.
  Ask, don't tell : powerful questioning in the classroom / Angela Peery, Polly Patrick, Deb Moore.
     pages cm
  Includes bibliographical references and index.
  ISBN 978-1-935588-42-9 (alk. paper)
  1. Questioning.   I. Patrick, Polly, author.   II. Moore, Deb, author.   III. Title.
  LB1027.44.P44 2013
  371.3'7—dc23
                                                                    2013007550

ISBN 978-1-935588-42-9
Printed in the United States of America

17 16 15 14 13   01 02 03 04 05 06 07

CONTENTS

༝ঌၜ

LIST OF FIGURES

∽○∼

ABOUT THE AUTHORS

Angela Peery, Ed.D., is a Senior Professional Development Associate at The Leadership and Learning Center and works internationally, mainly in the area of instruction. Her varied experience includes more than 10 years of classroom teaching, four years as a high school assistant principal, and various leadership positions at the building, district, and state levels. She has taught undergraduate and graduate courses in both education and English, and has been a codirector of a National Writing Project site. She has published five books, including *Writing Matters in Every Classroom* (2009) and *The Data Team Experience: A Guide for Effective Meetings* (2011). Angela also generated several professional development seminars and accompanying materials for The Center, including the *Writing to Learn* series and *Power Strategies for Effective Teaching.*

Polly Patrick splits her time between being a classroom teacher and serving as a Teacher Instructional Coach for the Minnetonka Public Schools in Minnetonka, Minnesota. She also is an Adjunct Instructor at the University of St. Thomas and a Professional Development Associate at The Leadership and Learning Center. Polly has intentionally stayed in the classroom with high school students throughout her career. Recently, Polly has also served as a Staff Development Specialist for new teachers. In the last five years, Polly has been involved in the Instructional Leadership Team and the Grading and Reporting Committee that have been at the core of creating a learning culture at Minnetonka High School. Polly has traveled to multiple districts and national conferences promoting the value of creating grading systems that give an accurate reflection of what students know and can do. This is her first book publication.

Deb Moore earned her undergraduate degree in elementary education with a mathematics minor at Alverno College in Milwaukee, Wisconsin. After working in several K–8 schools, first as a teacher and then as a mathematics coach, she went back to Alverno to pursue a graduate degree with licensure as a director of curriculum and instruction. Deb spent a decade in the Elmbrook School District, Wisconsin, where she taught 8th-grade math before moving into the role of instructional coach. She left Elmbrook in June 2012 and moved to the east coast, where she just accepted a full-time position at the Urban Teacher Center in Baltimore. Deb is a clinical faculty member teaching elementary mathematics courses to preservice teachers and serves as a coach to a small cohort of her students with a mathematics emphasis as they complete their fieldwork and student teaching in urban elementary classrooms throughout Baltimore and Washington, D.C. This is her first book publication.

ACKNOWLEDGMENTS

❦

Angela Peery

I would like to thank the following exemplary educators for their significant contributions to this book: Angela Binkley, Carissa DeYoung, Amy Fast, Hayley Hook, Kourtney Ferrua, Leanne Geary, Robin Handloser, Annie Kelsey, Camilla Sutherland, Pat Flattley, and Majalise Tolan. This book would not be a reality without you.

All the educators across America who have worked with The Leadership and Learning Center's seminar *Power Strategies for Effective Teaching* are sincerely thanked for helping me inquire, research, and clarify my thinking about powerful questioning. In particular, McMinnville schools and Lincoln County schools in Oregon have been very influential.

My colleagues at The Center have been wonderful in supporting this work. Specifically, thanks go to Kristin Anderson, Lisa Cebelak, Jess Engman, and Tracey Shiel.

To my coauthors, Polly and Deb, you did it! You are now published!

Lastly, I thank my husband, Tim, for all he does each week while I'm on the road and in the air. He keeps everything running smoothly and also serves as a sounding board for all my ideas. Every time I hold this book in my hands, I know I will feel his presence on every page.

Polly Patrick

Thanks to all of the teachers who generously contributed ideas and practices from their classroom experiences. Lisa Carlson, Abram Jacobs, Josh Bettes, Kim Hoehne, Connie Strand, Eric Sill, Caleb Lee, Chris Pears, Brent Veninga, Blair Valone, Cheryl Smith, Tim McGraw, Jenny Van Aalsburg, Heather Markert, Joan George, Eileen Voth, and

Sara Lueth went the extra mile. You make the learning real; you are examples of the best in education.

Working at The Leadership and Learning Center is a new joy for me. Thank you to many there who have encouraged me and this work, especially Kristin Anderson, Jess Engman, Lisa Cebelak, and Jeff Erickson. A special thanks to coauthor Angela Peery, who initially encouraged me to pursue working with The Center.

Thanks to my amazing family. From the beginning, our now adult children, Lance and Megan, have made life so rich; they make questioning an art form. And when I thought it couldn't get better, my children both chose to marry teachers, Lisa and Abram. Thanks to Mark, my husband of more than 40 years, and my personal therapist, extraordinary editor, and consummate cheerleader; I am so grateful!

Deb Moore

I would like to thank the teachers I have worked with over the years; I have been very fortunate to work with some very talented, dedicated educators. I would also like to thank my husband, Bill, and four children, Stephanie, Melissa, Peter, and Sam. There have been a lot of pizza deliveries made during these last few months, but there have been no complaints. Their support has been amazing. (Or perhaps they prefer the delivery pizza to my cooking!) Either way, thank you so much!

CHAPTER 1

Questions Are an Invitation to Learn and to Connect

⁓୦⌒

"It's not the answer that enlightens, but the question."

Eugene Ionesco

Asking questions comes naturally to all of us. A typical day for the average person is filled with both questions and answers, as these are at the heart of communication. Artful questioning may also be the most powerful tool teachers have in their instructional toolkits. Teachers' questions help them manage their classes, engage students with the subject matter, encourage dialogue, and deepen understanding. This chapter will examine the power of questions to invite others to learn and to provide human connection.

Questions Are an Invitation to Learning

"Why?"

Those who have been around small children know this question well. We learn quickly that when answered, it most often generates a second question: "Why?" The race is on until eventually the adult tires of answering and says "Just because," and the child toddles off to the next "big person" who may or may not be excited to engage in the same type of conversation. In this familiar scenario, we can find one of the core motivations for this book.

A child, consciously or not, learns two truths about questions. The first is that the child's brain is simply doing what comes naturally—showing curiosity, experiencing the new discoveries all around, and finding patterns in the world. The second truth, just as critical, is that the child can find human connection by engaging another person in the questioning. The child issues an invitation, and the adult receives and responds to that invitation by answering. Through questioning, the child satisfies a critical human need—connection. Let's examine these two aspects of questioning more closely.

Questions Remind Us that We Are Wired to Learn

Neuroscience helps us understand more about our brain's use of questioning. We process information in two ways: bottom-up processing and top-down processing. It is great fun to watch psychology students come to realize this through a classroom activity. You can try it with the following activity.

QUESTION: *What do you see?*

When doing this activity in the classroom, after several responses, a student discovers that there is a Dalmatian sniffing the ground in the center of the picture. A next step can be to ask everyone in the class to find the Dalmatian. There is noisy collaboration until all students have focused on the target.

The first question of this series initiated bottom-up processing. This is a more primal response, when all of the senses work to find something of interest. In other words, the interpretation or response emerges from the data.

Once the search for the Dalmatian begins, top-down processing takes over. In this instance, the processing involves a conscious choice to focus on a target once the target is announced. Top-down processing occurs any time that stated expectations influence the interpretation of the basic sensory data.

When using top-down processing we are answering the question, "What do I want to concentrate on?" When a learner intentionally chooses, he always focuses better. Being curious is part of the hard-wiring of the brain. The search for the Dalmatian always drives a flurry of conversation.

When teachers invite students to engage in learning, the brain moves into action. A strong question taps into the brain's natural curiosity and invokes engagement. Then questions are not just about "schoolwork" but rather about learning, thinking, and interacting in the moment.

Questions Connect Us

Consider for a moment a common but extremely important question: "Will you marry me?" What a powerful moment that is for the two involved! Now it's not just a small child questioning why; it's an adult asking another adult a life-altering question. This critical question connects two people, families, and groups of friends, touching a myriad of other people. The answer sets the rest of one's life in motion.

As we ask questions and wait for the answers, we form a bond with other people. A question is part of a reciprocal relationship; it demands an answer. The amygdala in the brain is active when we talk about the emotional connection in the marriage question. Sometimes neural connections are about the emotion; sometimes the connections can be finding a pattern that the brain is also looking for, as was discussed earlier with the bottom-up and top-down processing.

In classrooms where the climate encourages and respects questions, there is no end to the connection possibilities. Questions in these classrooms build relationships between the teacher and students and among the students as they listen to each other exchange both questions and answers. Beyond the relationships between people, questions also encourage students to make new connections to concepts and ideas within a discipline.

Questions have been key to good teaching forever. Socrates knew the value of questions. He used six types of questions to engage students in learning because he understood that it is the dialogue that helps each person construct meaning and connect with both the material and each other. "Sitting with" questions and allowing them to guide conversations is the core of the Socratic method, which is still used effectively in classrooms from the early grades through adult education all over the world.

Many of today's prominent educational leaders highlight the importance of generating and asking critical questions.

Parker Palmer, who writes extensively about the heart of teaching and learning, has a vision of creating a community in every classroom. Both in his early work, *To Know as We Are Known* (1993), and later in *The Courage to Teach* (1997), he speaks of creating space where the teacher acts as the host, practicing hospitality when inviting students to learn and to question. He says, "A learning space needs to be hospitable not to make learning painless, but to make the painful things possible, things without which no learning can occur—things like exposing ignorance, testing tentative hypotheses, challenging false or partial information, and mutual criticism of thought" (Palmer, 1997, p. 74). The ideal learning community calls for a trusting classroom climate that allows for real conversations that connect teachers and learners as they do the personal work of learning together.

John Hattie (2012) provides a useful reminder for all teachers about the amount of teacher talk versus student talk. He calls for teachers to engage in dialogue, not monologue. In a monologue, few questions are used except for a rhetorical question here and there. In a dialogue, many questions are asked that invite students into the current dialogue and also into the learning process itself. This is when the learning is understood, and the class works together as a community. Each member moves beyond merely taking in information; one is able to talk about learning and, in turn, demonstrate evidence of higher student achievement. Questions are at the core of this type of learning.

As cited in *Classroom Instruction That Works* (Marzano, Pickering, and Pollock, 2001), Redfield and Rousseau found back in the 1980s an effect size of 0.73 for students who were exposed to high-level questions. Robert Marzano, one of the authors of this seminal work, also urges teachers to use "elaborative interrogation," which consists of using questions that ask, "Why would that be true?" (Marzano, 2007, p. 38). Just keeping in mind the simple question "Why would that be true?" could be incredibly helpful when orchestrating class discussion and facilitating interaction among students during periods of questioning.

Michael Schmoker, another education reformer, is well known for using pointed questions. In *Results Now* (2006), he asks, "What do we see in the vast majority of classrooms?" His answer: "We find startling amounts of busy work, with no connection to important standards or common curriculum." Schmoker has modeled for us the courage to ask the probing, uncomfortable questions that demand answers for the sake of our students. Countless book study groups have held critical conversations around the questions in his books.

The bottom line is that while "telling" may seem more efficient, "asking" and interacting are where the relationship of learning between teacher and student is built. Where there is powerful questioning, there is a powerful and productive community of learners.

Questions Are Key to Educational Change and Transformation

Education has been reawakened to the need for evidence, partially by the role evidence-citing plays in the Common Core State Standards. Additionally, a growing frustration with the amount of "test prep" that students do as schools grapple with No Child Left Behind legislation has led educators, students, and families to demand less "multiple choice thinking." Higher-level questions demand more than multiple-choice answers, both verbally and in writing. Good teachers have always known this.

Thinking is at the core of improving instruction, and questions often are the catalysts that focus that thinking. This book will provide supportive research throughout, but here are a few highlights of questions that teachers ask of students:

- Jay McTighe and Grant Wiggins (2005) have promoted "backwards design" and creating essential questions. In their work, the core of the unit is the essential question that states what the students will work to answer.

- Larry Ainsworth (2003) has written much about what he calls Essential Questions and their corresponding Big Ideas. In short, Essential Questions are those guiding, inviting questions that frame units and lessons and invite students into the learning. Big Ideas are the "a-ha" realizations and long-lasting learning that students gain from participating in the units and lessons.

• John Hattie seeks to bring together the evidence that demonstrates effective practices that classrooms use to ensure student success in *Visible Learning* (2009) and *Visible Learning for Teachers* (2012). Questioning, student-teacher relationships, formative assessment, metacognitive strategies, reciprocal teaching, feedback, classroom discussion, and problem-solving teaching all appear in the top 25 out of 150 influences on student achievement. Each of these depends on quality questions. There is also research that focuses on questions that teachers need to ask of themselves and of each other.

• Douglas Reeves (2010) has said that the essential question for teams of teachers is, "What can we do tomorrow to help students and teachers achieve their goals?" This question should drive the work that collaborative teacher teams do on a daily basis.

• Richard DuFour and Robert Eaker (1998) have framed much of the dialogue around professional learning communities with these four questions: What do we expect students to learn? How will we know if they are learning? What will we do when students are already proficient? How do we respond when students don't learn? Schools and school systems have been trans-formed as they have used these questions to guide the work of instruction.

• Michael Fullan has used questions as a basis of his work on change and has even used them to form titles of books, including *What's Worth Fighting For in the Principalship?* (2008).

- Charlotte Danielson (2007) sees questions as so central that they are included in the four domains in her framework that is used by so many teacher evaluation systems to examine work in classrooms. One of the key practices that is considered in domain three is the quality of the questions the teacher asks.

These are just a few of the highlights of work being done throughout education these days that calls us to question and reflect on our questioning techniques in the classroom and with each other as educators. When we as teachers ask and seek answers to the tough questions, then we are more ready to share with passion the central role of questions in the process of learning. Teachers who are excited about learning have students who are excited as well, because it's easy to share excitement when we have it in abundance.

Questions are Powerful Strategies for Teachers Who Want to Reach Their Students

Teachers don't just "get" an understanding of the power of questions because we ask so many—literally hundreds per day, as documented over the past few decades by numerous researchers (Leven and Long, 1981; Pollock, 2007). Nor do students just "get" an understanding about content or learning just because they show up in class. When students own and discuss their learning, they become what John Hattie often calls "self-regulated learners." As Hattie (2012) notes, "When students can … self-regulate their learning, they can use feedback more effectively to reduce discrepancies between where they are in their learning and the desired outcomes or successes of their learning. Such feedback—usually in the form of reflective or probing questions—can guide the learner on 'when,' 'where,' and 'why' in selecting or employing task- and process-level knowledge and strategies" (p. 120).

Teachers want empowered learners leaving their classrooms at the end of their time together. That empowerment will happen as the dialogue between teachers and students and between students and their peers becomes stronger. Dialogue improves as teachers ask questions and deeply listen to the answers.

Studying the art of powerful questions is not for the faint-hearted. It is because of that complexity that many teachers retreat, because there is already so much to think about every day in the classroom. We encourage you to continue studying questioning because the use of effective questions can have such a huge impact. And, as students take on asking their own questions of each other, the teacher's work becomes not only "easier," but also more satisfying. Students become so engaged when they get to ask their own questions. John Hattie's "mantra" is that successful, engaged learning occurs when "teachers see learning through the eyes of the students and students become their own teachers" (Hattie, 2012).

In *Making Thinking Visible* (Ritchhart, Church, and Morrison, 2011), the authors build a case for several thinking "moves." They have the reader think through learners who may come to an understanding at different points. They point out, "Thinking doesn't happen in a lockstep, sequential manner, systematically progressing from one level to the next. It is much messier, complex, dynamic, and interconnected than that. This is intricately connected to content; and for every type or act of thinking, we can discern levels or performance" (p. 8).

The authors discuss the following moves that a learner undertakes when thinking to learn (p. 13):

1. Observing closely and describing what's there

2. Building explanations and interpretations

3. Reasoning with evidence

4. Making connections

5. Considering different viewpoints and perspectives

6. Capturing the heart and forming conclusions

7. Wondering and asking questions

8. Uncovering complexity and going below the surface of
   things

We count on students emulating the questioning skills that they see and experience from their teachers as they interact with their peers. In this way, they learn what Marzano and Heflebower (2012) call "conative" skills as opposed to cognitive skills. The cognitive skills are those used to analyze and utilize information; the conative skills are those used to understand and control oneself.

They go on to say of the skills that in the 21st century, these conative skills are "particularly important and must be taught because communication with a wide variety of people, many of whom hold very different opinions and interpretations, is now commonplace. Students must be able to understand multiple interpretations in order to communicate successfully" (p. 23). We, the authors of this book, contend that thoughtful questioning is how this work is done. The more intentional a teacher is about using questions in the classroom, the greater the chance that students will learn to become fluent in both their cognitive work and conative work.

"What does powerful questioning look like in the classroom?" is the driving question for this book. We will attempt to describe effective questioning through both exposition and narration, using vignettes of teacher practice. Our focus is on those moments when teachers and students are engaged in classroom questioning tasks that involve face-to-face interactions and oral discourse, as this is what comprises the great majority of time spent in schools.

VIGNETTE

QUESTIONING AND READ-ALOUDS

By Amy Fast, Teacher and Instructional Coach

When we talk about questioning in school, most of us picture the teacher standing in front of the class, asking questions and waiting for students to respond. However, powerful questioning can be used in many ways. It can be the driving force of a unit or lesson, a means of assessing or checking for deep understanding, and the lens through which we read and write.

If you ask elementary teachers about our favorite part of the day, we will often respond that it is the read-aloud that we enjoy the most. When you pry a little further you will find out that it is so enjoyable because it is a time when we can talk about life lessons with students and read together purely for enjoyment. A few years ago, under pressure to make sure that every second of the teaching and learning in my 5th-grade classroom was intentional, focused, and getting the biggest bang for its buck (hitting as many standards as I could as deeply as possible), I found myself grappling with what to do about read-aloud. Sure, it is a great time to model fluent reading and thinking about the text, but is it worth the twenty minutes I had been spending on it?

Refusing to give up something I knew in my heart was meaningful, I decided that the only thing I could do was make it *more* meaningful. Powerful questioning would be where I would start. At the time we were reading *Holes*, by Louis Sachar, and I knew that the students were enthralled with the story. I also knew, though, that we could take it a lot deeper if we tried. At the beginning of the next day's reading I posed the question to students, "Are people *all* good or *all* bad?" and then I had them open their notes journals and make a T-chart. At the top they copied down my question. I had them title the left-hand column "text" and the right-hand column "thoughts." Their assignment was to find examples from the text as we read that could help them answer the question, and then write down their thoughts about those parts of the text they chose.

The first day I modeled for them, taking notes and thinking aloud as I read, and as the week continued, they got the hang of it. On Friday, we set aside a time to discuss the reading. I posed the question that had been guiding our reading for the week to the students and what followed floored me. Students were chomping at the bit to discuss the reading, citing the text was happening organically, and students were making connections and inferences that I don't think I would have elicited had I posed the question without having them take notes about it throughout. Their notes were a means of processing and synthesizing the question and how the text pertained to it.

I started using note-taking throughout more of the day, always starting by posing a powerful question for the students to be thinking about and writing about as they were learning. They used note-taking during independent reading with questions like, "Is the author effective at getting you interested in the characters? Why or why not?" They did quick writes about the powerful question, sometimes as lesson closure, using their notes as an outline. Every subject of every day started with a powerful question and every subject of every day students were expected to take notes and write about their learning.

At the end of the year we read the young readers' edition of *The Omnivore's Dilemma,* by Michael Pollan, during our read-aloud time. I posed the same question every day to the students — "Should I be more thoughtful about what I eat?" — and every day students took notes using examples from the text to answer that question. When we finished the book, students had a whole journal full of notes and research that addressed that one powerful question. I had them go through and highlight their notes on the text and their thoughts about the text that they felt were the most powerful arguments about whether or not they should be more thoughtful about what they eat.

The students then *asked me* if they could write argumentative essays that I could pass on to the school board. Of course I complied, and guided them through the process. All of them started with the thesis, "I should be more thoughtful about what I eat," and most of them convincingly supported their arguments by citing many points in the text, including research about school lunches. The essays were anywhere from three to seven pages long, and they were all on topic and organized . . . and these were fifth graders!

As I put the finished essays in an envelope to send to the district office I couldn't help but reflect on how my read-aloud had changed. It became so much more meaningful and motivating through the use of writing and powerful questioning, and that small change rippled through the rest of my instruction so that those two components were at the core of everything we did in our classroom. Needless to say, students were constantly engaged, processing their learning, and achievement was at an all-time high.

CHAPTER 2

Powerful Questions Can Work Wonders

❦

"It is better to know some of the questions than all of the answers."

James Thurber

"More effort needs to be given to framing questions that are worth asking..."

John Hattie
(2012, p. 75)

Often the pressure of "covering the curriculum" interferes with teachers' desires to engage students in the most powerful learning opportunities possible. As springtime nears, and brings along with it a battery of assessments, teachers find themselves rushing and overloading students with drills and practice, mind-numbing lectures, and barrages of recall-level questions. Educators do this with the best intentions: they want students to be successful and are trying to provide them with every last tidbit of information, hoping that details or skills that have never "stuck" before will somehow, this time, "stick."

We educators must break our pattern of pelting students with low-level question after low-level question, day after day—not just as the school year draws to a close. John Hattie (2009), who has conducted the most comprehensive meta-analysis of factors that influence student learning, is only the latest researcher to present the shocking facts: 60 percent of the questions teachers ask about the content of the lesson are recall-level, and another 20 percent of questions are procedural or behavioral. He notes that most teachers' questions, both verbal and written, relate only to surface knowledge, and in some studies, recall-level questions comprised 80 percent of the questions asked (p. 182). The reality is simple. Powerful questioning techniques are essential if students are to master the content and skills necessary for success in academia, the workplace, and in life.

What Is a Powerful Question?

We have established that questions are central to learning because inquiry and wonder are wired into humans' brains. We have looked at how questions can be the invitation to strong connections within a learning community. It's now time to define and explore what constitutes a powerful question.

When in doubt, previous generations would look in a dictionary for definitions. That is what we do here as well (http://dictionary .reference.com/browse/question?s=b):

> **Question (*noun*)**
>
> 1. A sentence in an interrogative form, addressed to someone in order to get information in reply.
> 2. A problem for discussion or under discussion; a matter for investigation.
> 3. A matter of some uncertainty or difficulty; problem (usually followed by *of*): *It was simply a question of time.*
> 4. A subject of dispute or controversy.
> 5. A proposal to be debated or voted on, as in a meeting or a deliberative assembly.

These definitions directly align with the critical features we have already examined. In the first, we see the power of human connection, or questioning as invitation. Questioning is reciprocal; the person asking does not do so in isolation, but in order to engage another's mind and/or emotions.

In the second definition, we see the idea of the exploration our brain does when we are involved in bottom-up and top-down processing. Definition two highlights the human predisposition to analyze, collaborate, and inquire.

Definitions three, four, and five get at the heart of academic and civic education, and have direct ties to the main thrusts of the Common Core State Standards, which are going to be a driving force in instruction and assessment in the United States for at least the next decade. Logical reasoning, valid claims and conclusions, and fruitful collaboration are threads that run through all the currently released Common Core standards, so words like "dispute," "debated," and "deliberative" should strike a chord with educators.

It should now be clear that one of the big ideas we want to emphasize in this book is that powerful questions are collaborative in nature. A curious mind may obviously create endless questions—but the most powerful questions are created and answered in partnership with other curious minds.

We also see in all of the definitions above the implication that the question engages the person or people seeking to answer it. So, the second big idea we want to emphasize about powerful questions is that they engage the learner. In other words, the learner is intrigued by the questions and earnestly seeks answers through metacognition, discourse, research, collaboration, and other methods.

Let's go deeper into defining engagement. What do we mean by engagement? Briefly, for educational settings, we mean: "students attending to and participating in the learning task at hand." The students' actions are more than symbolic compliance, and include behaviors such as using active listening, freely offering ideas in class discussions, and writing original compositions on topics of study and/or interest (Peery, 2009, p. 116).

Increasing student engagement, then, is a huge part of becoming better at our questioning techniques as teachers. Lack of student engagement is an enormous problem in the United States, and abroad as well. For example, in the U.S., Learning 24-7 conducted an extensive study in 2004 that documented approximately 82 percent of classrooms with fewer than half the students engaged in instruction at the times of the observations (Peery, 2009, p. 57). A report called *The Silent Epidemic* (Bridgeland, Dilulio, and Morison, 2006) reported that 47 percent of high school dropouts said their classes "weren't interesting," and that this was a major factor in their departures (Peery, 2009, p. 84). Pianta, Belsky, Houts, and Morrison (2007) reported after a study of 2,500 elementary school classrooms that students spent more than 90 percent of class time listening to the teacher or working alone; they spent only 7 percent of classroom time working in groups. Additionally, teachers spent the bulk of their time lecturing and very little time giving individual feedback.

Engagement is critical to achievement. John Hattie (2012) has reported that disengaged students achieve only about the same as students who are classified as "highly disruptive."

Engagement also means that everyone is involved in the learning; in other words, there is "no opt out," a term used in the book *Teach Like a Champion* (Lemov, 2010). This is a phrase that has wider implications than the name and the description in the book imply. Shouldn't any classroom be a place in which dialogue is expected? Some of us may have experienced a true dialogic classroom only a few times in our lives. It has been said that classroom participation and discussion are done well in only two places in American education— kindergarten and graduate school. You may chuckle as you read that statement—but you may also be nodding in agreement.

We, the authors of this book, believe it is not okay for high school students to choose to sit in the very back of the room and stare out the windows, lay their heads on their desks, or actively disrupt the learning of others. It is also not okay for students to say "I don't know" when asked a question, or to simply shrug their shoulders. It is not okay for teachers to call only on those students who raise their hands or blurt out answers. It is not okay for sedate girls to be answering most of the questions while wiggly boys are reprimanded for their behavior but not asked what they are thinking. In the classroom where powerful questioning is the norm, full engagement by all is demanded by the teacher. Every word and action of the teacher works in harmony with this expectation.

A third big idea about powerful questions is that they immediately engender deep, diverse, creative, or metacognitive thinking. In some cases, lower-level, prerequisite questions may precede the more powerful questions, but we should perhaps keep in mind the reminder from Marzano, Pickering, and Pollock (2001) to use inferential and analytic questions as often as possible. In general, these questions move beyond the "who," "what," and "when" to ask "why" and "how" instead.

We must be mindful of the research that shows that students whom teachers perceive as slow or poor learners are asked fewer higher-cognitive questions than students perceived as more capable learners (Rosenthal and Jacobson, 1966). This bias often goes undetected by teachers, and it greatly impacts the quality of instruction, not only for struggling learners, but for the entire classroom.

In the book *Making Thinking Visible* (Ritchhart, Church, and Morrison, 2011), the authors note that the simple question "What makes you say that?" is "one of the most fully integrated thinking routines" in classrooms of teachers who are dedicated to improving their understanding of students' thinking (p. 34). This single question, asked repeatedly as students engage in classroom discourse, can vastly improve the quality of teachers' questions and the quality of students' answers. This question could be the beginning of any teacher's journey toward lessening the focus on the "one right answer" and better understanding students' reasoning and misconceptions.

How Are Questions Classified?

Bloom's *Taxonomy of Educational Objectives* (1956) is the most commonly known classification of cognitive complexity in education. The original six levels have been part of lesson planning for decades:

- Knowledge—recalling or recognizing information
- Comprehension—understanding and manipulating information in a basic way; explaining, comparing, classifying, describing
- Application—using the knowledge and skills that have been gained in new, concrete situations
- Analysis—using inductive and deductive reasoning to discern component parts and uncover relationships
- Synthesis—thinking originally and creatively; creating something new, using what was learned; putting component parts together to form a new whole
- Evaluation—judging the merit, worth, or value of an idea, aesthetic work, solution to a problem, etc.

In 2001, Anderson and Krathwohl published a revision of this original taxonomy that was intended to update the work for the 21st century. Briefly, the taxonomy became two-dimensional, with knowledge classified as either factual, conceptual, procedural, or metacognitive. These knowledge dimensions are then considered in relation to the cognitive processes, now designated as remember, understand, apply, analyze, evaluate, and create. Most educators quickly note that the top two levels seem to be the reverse of the original, but this is a simplistic interpretation. The cognitive process levels are further divided into other categories, so this update to the original is actually quite a bit more complex. A matrix of the four knowledge dimensions and the six cognitive process dimensions would contain 24 cells.

We, the authors, find that teachers are generally not using the revised taxonomy but are still planning with the older one in mind. This is not a criticism as such, but just a recognition of current practice. We do, however, advocate that educators engage in an "unwrapping" process (Ainsworth, 2003) or backward design process with the Common Core standards and/or any other standards or objectives they are required to use for unit and lesson planning.

In 1999, Norman Webb, a mathematics educator at the Wisconsin Center for Education Research, created the Depth of Knowledge (DOK) model, which is increasingly being used by educators as they grapple with the rigor of the Common Core State Standards. The DOK model examines the depth of knowledge required for meeting standards and/or being successful on an assessment task. The DOK model has four levels: recall, skill or concept, strategic thinking, and extended thinking. The DOK level is determined by examining the task the student has to perform in relation to the thinking that occurs.

We find that educators in only a few states know the DOK model well and are using it in their instructional planning; therefore, in this book, we will most often reference Bloom's Taxonomy. However, we do encourage practitioners to learn more about Webb's DOK as it becomes more prominent in the discourse educators have about the Common Core standards.

Using Questions to Engage Students, Clarify Thinking, and Deepen Understanding

These three purposes, which may or may not be distinct from each other at any given time, are suggested as a "frame" for powerful questioning in a book called *Make Just One Change: Teach Students to Ask Their Own Questions* (Rothstein and Santana, 2011). In this section, we will provide our own discussion of these purposes.

"Actively processing information is the beginning point of learning," Robert Marzano aptly notes (2007, p. 59). A prerequisite for active processing is gaining the mental attention of students. A disengaged student cannot benefit from even the best questions, because his or her mind is not on the task or "in the game."

Marzano summarizes pertinent research on engagement and achievement and indicates that engagement can increase achievement by as much as 31 percentile points (2007, p. 99).

Obviously, the issue of engagement is a complex one, and it grows more complex as our world becomes increasingly technology-rich and globally connected. There is simply so much more to pay attention to, for students and for teachers, and thus, focusing on the topic at hand and engaging in academic discourse for much of a class period demands that teachers use their best techniques for engaging students.

Marzano (2007, pp. 100–103) recommends several specific stimuli for engaging students in classroom instruction in general; these can also be applied to questioning, and are as follows:

- High energy
- Missing information
- The self
- Mild pressure
- Mild controversy

By high energy, Marzano means the quick pacing of instruction, including "teacher intensity," physical activity, and brisk pacing (2007, p. 100). As far as using missing information, Marzano cites natural human curiosity and suggests a specific strategy, clozentropy (p. 101). Clozentropy, often used in what is commonly known as "cloze reading," is the omission of words in text, which triggers the brain to search for the missing information. In terms of the self as stimulus, Marzano discusses personal interest and efficacy (p. 102).

Mild pressure applies directly to periods of questioning and discussion, because, as Marzano says, "If students realize that there is a moderate chance of being called on to answer a question, it will likely raise their level of attention" (2007, p. 103). This particular stimulus directly applies to the initial engagement of students in questioning. Each teacher needs to create a classroom culture of learning in which there is *always* mild pressure to participate—that's fundamental to engendering dialogue.

Marzano's idea of mild controversy also applies to the initial engagement of students in periods of questioning. Questions worth discussing at length are often provocative. Structured academic debate, Socratic discussion, and other specific techniques can meet the criteria for either mild pressure or mild controversy and thus enhance engagement overall.

So, where does a teacher begin? We must capture each student's mental attention, form questions, facilitate discussion, and provide feedback to students between questions in order to keep the learning going forward during periods of classroom discussion. In terms of written questions to which students respond, we must also frequently design questions that are engaging enough for students to want their voices and answers heard or read.

There are, at a minimum, two parts relevant to engaging the learner—the question and the context in which the question is asked.

Both of these parts, however, presume that an effective learning environment has been established.

It is important to consider both the question and the context when planning the questions that will be asked and when considering classroom management techniques that will keep classroom discourse moving. Good questions engage the student both cognitively and socially. Ideally, even students reluctant to engage will engage, because it is both interesting and fun to do so.

We must be mindful of the work of Lev Vygotsky (1978), in which he posited that social interaction is critical to personal cognitive development. We certainly see this in our classrooms as students who know more about a topic and are perhaps more verbal than their peers share their ideas in whole-class or small-group work and later, we see other children repeating and expanding upon those same ideas. Sometimes, as teachers, we can even become exasperated that a student hears a fellow student explain something and "gets it" readily, whereas we've been explaining the same exact thing repeatedly without such success. A situation like that, while frustrating, should shed light on how powerful student-to-student talk is for individual learning.

The technique "no opt out" (Lemov, 2010) mentioned earlier is worth examining in terms of engaging the learner. This technique is based upon the premise that it's not okay not to try (p. 28). This simple idea is at the core of high-performing classrooms in which the teachers absolutely believe that all students can learn and all students have something worthwhile to contribute. Basically, a "no opt out" sequence begins with a student unable to answer a question and ends with that student answering correctly (p. 28). The maneuvers the teacher makes within the sequence can vary, but what the teacher must constantly consider are the responses of the reluctant or disengaged student, the way those responses are handled, the contributions of fellow students, and how the sequence is moving learning ahead for *every* student.

Clarifying thinking is at the core of learning and is critical in order for formative assessment to work well for both teachers and students. Uncovering student misconceptions or surface-level understandings can only be done in classroom discourse if the prerequisite for engagement is met—and in order for that to happen, the teacher must have established a classroom culture of learning and planned worthwhile questions. Then, during the process of asking those questions, the teacher must constantly watch, listen, and respond; it is "real-time" formative assessment in every sense of the term.

Formative assessment at its best helps students find where their misconceptions are and what needs to change in their thinking. That kind of clarity comes more readily when we structure questions so that students can "hear" their own thinking, take it apart, and then put it back together, incorporating new learning. One can more easily hear his or her own thinking when it is articulated aloud and when it receives peer and teacher response. Often, we talk through our learning with a partner or small group so that we can incorporate ideas from others as we continue thinking. A skillful teacher's clarifying questions propel the classroom dialogue forward and also have the power to change an individual's thinking in many different ways.

Clarifying questions are sometimes distinguished from probing questions, but we lump these two together because we are discussing the clarifying or refining of cognition—not the clarifying of directions about the task, work groups, deadlines, and so on. We mean "clarify" in the original, basic meaning of the word: to make understandable or to free of confusion; to make something intelligible and/or to remove ambiguity.

The folks behind the excellent collection of educator resources online at Akron Global Polymer Academy have this to say about probing questions in science, but we feel that this text applies to all disciplines:

"Observers have found that recall-level questions pre-dominated even with teachers who were committed to fostering critical thinking. They refused to admit this until they saw documentation of their classroom behaviors.

"Probing questions, such as why?, can you elaborate?, what evidence can you present to support your answer? encourage students to 'unpack' their thinking, to show how they have reached particular conclusions. Teachers can use probing questions to press students to consider and weigh diverse evidence, to examine the validity of their own deductions and inductions, and to consider opposing points of view. Probing questions ask students to extend their knowledge beyond factual recall and 'parroting' of learned theories, to apply what is known to what is unknown, and to elaborate on what is known ...

"Probing questions contribute to a classroom climate of inquiry and thoughtful examination of ideas. Students who are regularly exposed to questions that force them to defend their responses with reasons and evidence may internalize this 'critical thinking' habit of mind." (http://agpa .uakron.edu/p16/btp.php?id=questioning)

Good probing questions have several characteristics, such as the following, which are offered for consideration but certainly not as an exhaustive list:

- Brevity—the teacher should not talk for very long; student dialogue must be furthered—this is not a time for a mini-lecture

- Divergence—multiple responses are possible

- Empowerment—the student is asked to continue the cognitive struggle; the teacher doesn't simply shift to another student, possibly a more eager one, or a faster auditory processor

• Reflection—the questions may cause students to make novel connections, or to be more metacognitive, or simply to pause and rethink what was already said

The third purpose of asking questions is to deepen understanding. The teacher is key to setting that climate for the interaction necessary for the "raw" thinking that students are doing at this point. Students often "draft" their answers off the teacher's attitudes and words. Students continue to stay engaged and thinking when our treatment of the answers is as important as the question itself.

At this level of questioning we want to be very aware of responding to students and not reacting to them. A reaction question might betray a bit of an edge in the voice, such as, "What did you just say?" or "Do you have *any* evidence for that?" A response, on the other hand, has no edge, and sounds more like, "Can you tell me more about your thinking about…?" "What have you read or heard that you are using for support?" Some of the edge is "just" tone, but tone represents attitude, and students thrive when there is a climate of acceptance. An attitude of arrogance or disdain, on the other hand, is deadly to true classroom dialogue.

Probing questions can help a student go beyond first-draft thoughts and the gathering of information, which is where many teachers feel the need to stop, because students have the facts and we must move on to "cover" the curriculum. Clarity of thought feeds students' interest and engagement, but to have questions be most helpful, teachers need to see asking questions (and receiving answers) as a process rather than a product.

In *Quality Questioning* (Walsh and Sattes, 2005), the process of answering a question has five steps (p. 78):

1. Listen to the question

2. Understand what is being asked for

3. Answer to self

4. Answer out loud, and sometimes,

5. Rethink and revise the answer

What does this process look like? Here is an example: Ms. Hoehne's physics class is trying to solve a momentum problem in collaborative groups. As Ms. Hoehne circulates from group to group, she asks:

• What is your process right now?

• Can you tell me what you're thinking right now?

• What's your plan?

• How did that work for you?

• What do your data show you?

• Are we stuck? or Where are we?

• What does the documentation show you?

Even her nonverbal actions are questions. She uses her eyes, posture, and hand movements to indicate a questioning climate. The dialogue around those questions is key to the students deepening their understanding.

Even though teachers don't know exactly what might happen in groups, like Ms. Hoehne, effective teachers anticipate and have plenty of questions ready. Questions, coupled with the five-step process suggested by Walsh and Sattes, establish the climate in which the students understand there will be genuine interest and response from the teacher as opposed to a reaction. Reactions always come at the risk of having students shut down their cognitive processing.

These steps and processes can begin with very young students and become a foundational skill necessary for older students both in the classroom and in life. The Common Core State Standards have included speaking and listening because of the power of articulating one's thinking. Questioning and thinking through the answers provide the building blocks of those skills in today's classrooms. If students experience an open climate in the interaction of questions and answers with the teacher, then that skill can transfer to their peers as well. During the time when each student is thinking, the teacher can't be everywhere, so it's advantageous for students to learn these thinking "moves" and to use them even without adult guidance.

Dylan Wiliam (2011) in *Embedded Formative Assessment* speaks of questions that a teacher would use as both discussion questions and diagnostic questions. Discussion questions can lead to an interesting class discussion if there is time. This is when the teacher is looking to bring out the *reason* for an answer, not just the fact. The students could get the fact correct, but not understand why they answered that way. Having the students engaged in the conversation and continuing to think is the key. This makes an effective discussion question.

If there is not time for the whole discussion, then a teacher may want to use a diagnostic question instead. These are questions designed to discover if the student has the correct answer for the correct reasons. Wiliam states that "the crucial feature of such diagnostic questions is based on a fundamental asymmetry in teaching; in general, it is better to assume that students do not know something when they do than it is to assume they do know something when they don't. What makes a question useful as a diagnostic question, therefore, is that it must be very unlikely that the student gets the correct answer for the wrong reason" (2011, p. 95).

In Ms. Carlson's biology class, a questioning scenario unfolded like this: The class was talking about evolution, and students were constructing their own definitions based on previous knowledge. This was a springboard into what would lead to evolution in the form of speciation. (Remember that the students have to have some level of knowledge when using a diagnostic question.)

Ms. Carlson asked, "Can you list as many things as you can think of that could potentially change the allele frequency of a population?" (This was the current working definition of evolution).

A student said, "What about genetic engineering?"

Ms. Carlson responded, "Can you tell me more about that?"

The same student replied, "If a particular organism is genetically modified to create a GMO [Genetically Modified Organism] in the lab, its allele frequency changes based on the genes that are added, subtracted, or modified."

Ms. Carlson followed with, "How would that technique lead to speciation?"

Another student then said, "If this GMO is planted or released into the wild, it could breed with other organisms and over time create a new species. Or if the gene modification influences a mating behavior or causes the species to reproduce at a different time than the rest of the species, it could lead to a new species."

The process of clarifying/probing continued until Ms. Carlson knew that the students got the right reason for the answer they were giving. Knowing the right reason is the heart of a diagnostic question.

In an elementary math lesson, diagnostic questions were used effectively as Mrs. Anderson posed this question to her students: Given the area and length of two adjoining rooms, determine the length of the connecting wall. Room A is 300 square feet with a length of 15 feet. Room B is 400 square feet with a length of 20 feet.

After a few minutes of students talking and working with self-selected partners on this task, one student offered, "I believe the length of the adjoining wall is 20 feet."

Mrs. Anderson replied, "Well, how do you know that?" She paused for a few seconds, looked at the rest of the class and asked, "How could we explain Seth's process to find an answer of 20 feet?"

A girl named Barbara answered, "First, he had to find the missing length of one room. We know that the total of one is 400 square feet and one of the dimensions is 20. So we would say that 20 times 20 is 400 and 15 times 20 is 300, so the adjoining wall is 20 feet."

Mrs. Anderson: "Okay, so Barbara and Timmy believe that the length of the wall is 20 feet. How could we draw a model of this problem to check their answer? I would like for each one of you to draw a model."

Mrs. Anderson circulated as students drew their models and coached students as necessary. At the end of the lesson, Mrs. Anderson had the class write a summary of their learning in their math journals.

What kind of question qualifies as a "deepening understanding question" in your content area? Think about forming questions that have two or more plausible answers, rather than questions that have just one right answer.

Deepening understanding is not a linear process. One of the important features of deepening understanding is making a prediction that one seeks to confirm. As Judith Willis, neurologist turned educator, writes, "Successful prediction is one of the best problem-solving strategies the brain has" (2008, p. 12). She tells of preschool children who learn important skills by asking questions and creating predictions in their playtime.

Robert Marzano says the situation that sets the stage for making predictions is centered on the invitation or questions posed. "Experimental inquiry is the quintessential task for generating and testing hypotheses" (2007, p. 91). That very experimental inquiry is where the questions take the lead. There are questions that the teacher first asks, but then, with training, the students follow closely with their questions as well.

To do this, there are two fundamental features that should be observed. The teacher and students must be engaged in dialogue with each other. The second follows closely; both parties must be listening to each other. The reason deepening understanding is harder is that it is difficult to script. So many educational leaders want to give teachers a checklist for classroom strategies—lists that look like recipes, with guaranteed success. This is just too simplistic.

Shirley Clarke talks about this interaction and active learning in her books, *Formative Assessment in Action* (2005) and *Active Learning through Formative Assessment* (2008). She says, ". . . the kinds of questions teachers ask determine how far the discussions will go in deepening and furthering children's learning and understanding" (2008, p. 51). She gives what she calls five templates for effective questions that reframe recall questions. They give us a starting point for how to ask questions that deepen understanding.

Clarke is quick to say that students must have some understanding before using these questions. However, look at the templates or ideas below and think about how they could possibly be applied in your teaching situation (Clarke, 2005, p. 68):

1. A range of answers—the teacher takes what would have been a recall question and reframes it, giving the students a range of possible answers. (These are similar to the diagnostic questions by Wiliam discussed earlier.) Example: What do you need to grow a flower? Possible answers: water, garden, seed, time, sunshine. (Clarke suggests including definite "yes" answers, definite "no" answers, and some ambiguous answers to enrich the discussion.)

2. A statement—turn a question into a statement and then ask if students agree or disagree. Students answer and give their reasons for their answers. Instead of asking which sport makes you think harder, you may say, "Basketball is the sport that makes you think the hardest. True or false?"

3. Right and wrong—two opposites are presented. Students are told that one is right and one is wrong. They have to decide and also explain how they decided. Example: In English language arts, give the students two sentences. Ask which is right and which is wrong, and then ask why, such as: "The boys wanted their ball. The boys wanted there ball."

4. Starting from the answer/end—give the answer and work backwards to how the student arrived at the answer. Instead of asking, "What is the answer to 2 + 3 + 4 − 1?" say, "Why is 8 correct, and what strategies do you use to know that?"

5. Opposing standpoint—a way to use a question to help a student see different perspectives or a different standpoint. Clarke had a fun example: Instead of asking, "How did Goldilocks feel when she saw the three bears' cottage?" ask, "How did the three bears feel upon discovering Goldilocks in their house?"

Shirley Clarke's templates give us excellent application ideas for asking questions.

In short, it is important to be prepared for the "messiness" of thinking when we are looking for deeper understanding. Questions are key to reaching that understanding.

Question Stems

Let's explore some additional examples of questions that lead to deeper understanding, from simple to more complex.

What if . . . ? This seems like a simple question—at least, it is easy to ask. This is a question that can be used with any age group, and its answers range from a few facts to a deep search for understanding.

So what? or *Now what?* Again, these seem like simple questions, but the answers allow students to build inferences, make predictions, or generate conclusions. They can even cause students to generate more questions of their own.

Making predictions. This is one of the roles in reciprocal teaching, because of its power. Teachers ask students to predict what happens next in a story, math problem, historical event, or experiment in science. The predictions help students make strong inferences and find evidence, a key skill in the Common Core State Standards.

Building Inferences. This, again, works with any age group. When teachers ask inferential questions, students make their own predictions and generate inferences. In *Classroom Instruction That Works* (Marzano, Pickering, and Pollock, 2001), there is support to help educators create inferential questions. The authors state, "When students access this 'right there' information, they do not have to think deeply about what they know; consequently, such questions do not elicit much prior knowledge or help students create a sturdy framework for learning new information. When teachers ask questions that require students to make inferences, however, students draw upon what they already know to 'fill in the blanks' and address missing information in the presented material" (2001, p. 54).

Some examples are given, including the following (2001, p. 55):

- For events—Who is usually involved in this event?

- For things and people—How is this thing usually used? Does this thing have a particular value?

- For actions—Who or what usually performs this action? How is the value of a thing changed by this action?

- For states of being—What are some of the changes that occur when something reaches this state?

Robert Marzano (2010) gives a clear process for students to analyze the effectiveness of their inferences in an article in *Educational Leadership*. He writes:

> "It [the process] involves posing four questions drawn from what researchers call *elaborative interrogation*. Typically, the teacher poses these questions to students and interacts with them around the answers. It's useful to examine both the truth of the premise and the validity of the thinking that led to the inference.
>
> 1. What is my inference?
> 2. What information did I use to make this inference?
> 3. How good was my thinking?
> 4. Do I need to change my thinking?"

Marzano concludes the article with, "Making inferences is the foundation to many of the higher-level thinking processes that we want students to use more effectively in the 21st century" (2010, p. 81).

We concur! Inferential questions asked by teachers get the students thinking. Students evaluating their inferences leads to even more learning.

Choosing an Interpretation. How do students form conclusions or choose an interpretation? Marzano and Heflebower (2012) include this in their book, *Teaching & Assessing 21st Century Skills*. They include it because "the act of consciously choosing one's own interpretation of events at any point in time might be the most powerful and useful skill regarding understanding and controlling oneself" (p. 125). Students need to know that they can think for themselves and have a great chance to change the outcome of any situation because of their thinking. There are four questions that they suggest for student use in this strategy.

1. What is my current interpretation of the situation?

2. What is the most likely outcome given my current interpretation?

3. Do I want a different outcome?

4. How must I change my interpretation to obtain a different outcome?

Learning the power of interpretation is key to promoting those conative skills discussed earlier. All of the questioning strategies used to help students deepen their understanding help students increase their thinking and learning not only about the content, but also about themselves as learners—and as people. When we work with students in this way, we promote a growth mindset as described by Dr. Carol Dweck (2006). Students moving toward a growth mindset vs. a fixed mindset is influenced greatly by their active interaction with the teacher and their peers about their thinking—which brings us to the last area of deepening understanding that we want to explore: metacognitive questions.

Metacognition and Questioning

Judith Willis (2008) helps educators understand the goal of metacognition, which is understanding and improving one's learning. Even very young children can learn a pattern of reflection that helps them become metacognitive. She says, "After a lesson or assessment, when children are prompted to recognize the successful learning strategies they used, that reflection can reinforce the effective strategies" (p. 281). Taking this time to respond to questions that help students reflect and practice metacognition needs to be seen as part of each lesson. Time becomes the enemy in the classroom, but if the combination of thinking and learning is the signature focus, then metacognitive questions need to be seen as a critical component for both teachers and students.

As was mentioned at the beginning of the section on deepening understanding, this is a process more than a product. This process is part of the gradual release of responsibility. Every time that students can put together "I used to think this" and "Now I think this" (Elmore, 2011) about their thinking they are moving toward learning that will be an incredible asset. Metacognition is an essential component of being able to identify both what and how we are learning.

John Hattie (2012) has ranked 144 influences on student achievement. He has ranked metacognitive strategies as high as 14th in a ranking of effective strategies to use with students, saying it has a 0.69 effect size. So how can teachers effectively work with students on metacognition?

Fisher and Frey (2008, pp. 28–29) use four power questions that they first found in N. J. Anderson's work (2002) to guide students as they move from cognition to metacognition:

1. What am I trying to accomplish?

2. What strategies am I using?

3. How well am I using the strategies?

4. What else could I do?

We suggest that these questions are good for both students and teachers. The power of the questions is in their ability to be catalysts that make us think, reflect, and continue to learn.

The best news it that there is always more to learn. In the following chapters of this book, you will find each discipline highlighted. The temptation is to read only about one's own discipline, but we assure you that the insights and strategies in each chapter can be adapted throughout the different disciplines. Each chapter also incorporates examples from across the age spectrum.

VIGNETTE
AUTHENTIC LITERACY
AND SOCRATIC SEMINAR
By an Instructional Coach

I was sitting in a 5th-grade class watching a teacher try Socratic seminar for the first time. A week earlier I had sent her some resources on Socratic seminar to look through so that she could understand the nonnegotiables and get helpful tips from teachers who had tried it before.

The students were sitting in two circles when I arrived. They had read a common, on-grade-level text that was engaging, and the teacher had gone over the expectations for students during the discussion—all important components of the instructional strategy.

As I watched the students attempt this authentic discussion, I felt for the teacher. In my experience, the first time students participate in Socratic seminar, it starts a little shaky. The teacher was shifting in her seat looking uncomfortable as her students were trying in vain to discuss the question she had prepared for them. The student conversation was stilted, and the same few students kept making the same remarks that sounded more like answers to multiple-choice questions than well-crafted points of view.

Quickly the teacher revealed the next question to students, trying to hurry along the discussion and keep students engaged. "What are some of the characteristics of the sister in the novel?" she asked. A few students (the same previously vocal students) took turns answering her question.

There was no student-to-student dialogue. This was going downhill fast.

She quickly glanced at me, her eyes pleading with me to help her turn this into what it was supposed to be—an engaging discussion about the reading, where students asked questions of each other, cited the text, shared differing points of view, connected the text to their own lives, and related to each other's experiences.

I thumbed through her lesson plan again. "Jump to the last question," I suggested.

In a last-ditch attempt, the teacher revealed the last question on the board and read it aloud, the hopelessness evident in her voice. "Is fear bad?"

Silence filled the room. After a few seconds she glanced at me again, this time with a little more panic.

"Wait," I mouthed to her from across the room.

She started tapping her foot and nervously looking around the circle of students, willing one of them to speak. Slowly, one of the students who hadn't participated yet began to speak: "Well, . . . I don't think it is all the time."

"Go on," the teacher prompted.

"Well, isn't fear what keeps us from running into the street?" he said tentatively.

Another student perked up. "Yeah, but fear doesn't feel good. Being scared is not fun. Scary movies are bad for kids, right?"

Then another student jumped in and added, "In the text the sister was very afraid and . . ."

And there it was. True discussion had begun.

Argumentative literacy is fundamentally reading about, writing about, and debating powerful questions that are motivating for students and essential to their understanding about the world in which they live. It is about students forming opinions and challenging others. It is about developing the skills to read in order to extract meaning, to write in order to persuade, and to speak in order to be heard. These are skills that students need in the real world, skills that are the essence of competing in a global society and of being an influential member of a democracy.

What is it that evokes such meaningful reading, writing, and discussion? Powerful questioning, as in this example. "Is fear bad?" has no easy answer.

Think about when you are most fired up and enjoy learning. It is when you are chatting with friends or colleagues about some controversial or provocative issue or when you are taking a stance or hashing out a problem that desperately needs solving. Because these discussions are meaningful to us, we work hard at honing our communication skills because we believe that our opinion not only matters but *could* make a difference if we present it well.

We want students to learn to read, write, and speak well in order for them to be able to make a difference. And if making a difference is so motivating and empowering, then we shouldn't be waiting until students leave school for their skills to make an impact. We should be asking powerful and universal questions: questions that require pondering, analyzing, reflecting, and researching; questions that evoke strong opinions; questions that relate to the world in which our students live and that motivate students to put in the effort that is required for them to come across as informed, articulate, and convincing. It is powerful questioning that puts the meaning in the reading, the fire in the discussion, and the motivation in the writing.

In the example I just shared, the powerful question was well crafted. Fear is a universal feeling, and those students clearly wanted to talk about it. Their continued reading became a catalyst to help them understand this complex emotion and to think differently about it in the future. Their discussion became a vehicle to learn from each other's experiences and points of view, and later, their writing became a means of convincing others that their thoughts were well developed and worthy of being heard.

I am gratified that I was there to support this teacher so that she didn't "give up" on Socratic discussion techniques.

CHAPTER 3

Powerful Questioning in English Language Arts

ꙮ

"For many years, teachers and researchers have known that students learn better and that their learning lasts longer in language-intensive classrooms. No matter what the subject, the people who read it, write it, and talk it are the ones who learn it best."

National Council of Teachers of English
(position statement, 1993)

Speaking and listening are at the heart of a good education in English language arts. Even the name indicates such, as we could not have the discipline itself without the word "language."

It has been established in this book that much of the talk occurring in classrooms is teacher-directed and is based upon low-level questions and procedural directives. As noted by many respected scholars in recent years, there is a lack of true academic discourse (Schmoker, 2011; Rose, 2005; Sizer, 1992; Powell, Farrar, and Cohen, 1986). It is the lack of effective classroom discussion in English language arts classes that is perhaps most disturbing to practitioners who have taught in this field for a number of years. If nowhere else, talk about timeless literature, the craft of writing, a valid argument, and so many other topics should dominate the "air time" in English language arts classes.

This chapter establishes the urgency for better questioning, both verbally and in writing, during English language arts instructional time. We also include ideas about how to craft better questions to use with reading, writing, and speaking/listening tasks and address the framework used throughout the book: engaging the learner, clarifying meaning, and deepening understanding.

Urgency

The United States is in a precarious situation as far as the literacy of its youth is concerned. Indeed, our literacy crisis was one of the compelling forces underlying the creation of the *Common Core State Standards for English Language Arts and Literacy in History/Social Studies, Science, and Technical Subjects.* Young people in the United States are no longer performing comparably to their global peers on most measures of reading and writing achievement, in addition to their more highly publicized low scores in science and mathematics.

Poor performance in literacy does not occur throughout all of the American educational system. For example, although students in grade 4 score among the best in the world, by grade 10, American students place close to the bottom among developed nations (OECD, 2006). Also, white students and students who are not poor achieve at a level more closely aligned to their counterparts in other nations than do American minority students of color and students who receive free or reduced lunch (NCES, 2006).

As students get older, it seems their achievement stagnates, or at least "wobbles." On the National Assessment of Educational Progress, for example, eighth and twelfth graders for almost 30 years have scored rather flatly in writing—with about three-quarters of them scoring consistently in the basic range (NCES, 2012).

Reading has not fared much better. Fourth-grade students have made small gains since 1992 (NCES, 2012). Our unscientific speculation is that the attention and funding given to early reading efforts may have been related. Unfortunately, however, fourth graders in 2011 scored the same as those in 2009. The average 8th-grade reading score in 2011 was only one point higher than in 2009, and five points higher than in 1992. Seniors have declined in reading performance. The average reading score for the nation's twelfth graders was two points higher in 2009, though, than in 2005; this is slightly encouraging. The score in 2009, however, was four points lower than the score for the first reading assessment in 1992. It seems that as American students get ready to exit the K–12 system and head to college and careers, their capabilities in reading are suspect. Driving forces behind the Common Core State Standards came to the same conclusion (Achieve, Inc., 2007; ACT, 2006; The National Commission on Writing, 2004).

American middle school and high school students with low literacy levels become students who either drop out before getting a diploma, or struggle mightily to earn a college degree, or populate the prisons. Graham and Perin (2007), two of the most prolific and respected researchers in adolescent literacy, have noted that weaker adolescent writers are less likely than their more skilled classmates to attend college. Then, when they get there, many weak students don't succeed. Advanced literacy skills across content areas is the best available predictor of students' ability to succeed in introductory college courses (Heller and Greenleaf, 2007). Yet, since the 1960s there has been a steady decline in the difficulty and sophistication of the content of the texts students have been asked to read (National Governors Association Center for Best Practices and Council of Chief State School Officers, 2010). And, as noted in one of Mike Schmoker's presentations (2009), "underdeveloped literacy skills are the number one reason why students are retained, assigned to special education, and given long term remedial services, and why they fail to graduate from high school."

For those who do manage to get a degree and secure employment, literacy demands do not cease. The demands continue. American businesses reportedly spend $3 billion annually on writing remediation (National Commission on Writing, 2004).

The Quality of Discourse in ELA Classrooms

There is quite a bit of disturbing evidence, some of which has already been cited in this text, about the lack of student talk in classrooms. If elementary students spend more than 90 percent of class time listening to the teacher or working alone, then how often are they engaging in discourse? If they spend only 7 percent of classroom time working in groups, how is productive academic talk even possible? Teachers spend the bulk of their time lecturing and very little giving individual feedback. If this study is any indication of what goes on in elementary classrooms, the outlook for secondary classrooms is even bleaker, as we, the authors of this book, generally see even less engagement in discussion and fewer instances of cooperative learning as the grade levels rise.

Oral language is of such importance in the early grades that it receives special attention in the Common Core State Standards and their accompanying documents. Appendix A notes:

> "If literacy levels are to improve, the aims of the English language arts classroom, especially in the earliest grades, must include oral language in a purposeful, systematic way, in part because it helps students master the printed word. Besides having intrinsic value as modes of communication, listening and speaking are necessary prerequisites of reading and writing." (p. 26)

Oral language, while perhaps taking a backseat to reading and writing skills in the higher grades, maintains some prominence in the Common Core standards, as one can easily see from a quick skim of the speaking and listening standards and also in examining the reading, writing, and language standards. A special note appears on page 48 of the ELA standards document, making clear the point that older students, too, need plenty of opportunity for productive talk: "Whatever their intended major or profession, high school graduates will depend heavily on their ability to listen attentively to others so that they are able to build on others' meritorious ideas while expressing their own clearly and persuasively" (National Governors Association Center for Best Practices and Council of Chief State School Officers, 2010).

A master teacher in Connecticut provided an excellent example of kindergarten academic discourse during one of Angela's visits to her school. The children had been read a picture book earlier and were engaged in snack time when Angela and the other observers arrived. Snack time was soon over, and the teacher (a veteran of 40 years) called the little ones back over to the reading rug and reminded them to sit "criss cross applesauce." She proceeded to remind them of the title of the story and said that she'd like for them to remember one of their favorite parts of the story and to be prepared to tell that part to a partner.

Within 30 seconds, she gave directions for the partners to talk, and they did, for a minute or two. Then this expert teacher called on various pairs to stand together. The first pair, two boys, stood. She called on one of the boys and said, "Now, I want you to tell everyone something your partner said. I know that you are all such good listeners."

The first student muttered a phrase or two, and she said, "Now Joshua, you know we need to show our guests what good speakers and listeners we are. Could you say what you said again, but this time, put it in a complete sentence, and say it nice and loud? Be proud!"

The boy beamed as he stated his sentence. Next, the teacher asked his partner, "Is that true, what Joshua said? Is that something you shared with him?" The second of the pair said, "Yes ma'am." The teacher then asked him if he could share something Joshua had told him.

This pattern went on for several pairs, until the children got fidgety. Each time a group stood, however, the teacher reminded them to speak in a complete sentence or two.

Now let's visit a high school classroom, in the same district as the kindergarten class that provided such a wonderful example of academic discourse. The teacher was conducting what appears to have been a grammar mini-lesson that morphed into a lengthy discussion of the appropriate use of the apostrophe with possessives and contractions (which, incidentally, is a skill that appears in the Common Core State Standards for second grade).

One young man in the class pointed to a sentence the teacher had modeled on the board and asked a question about the placement of the apostrophe, but called it "that thing . . . you know, that comma in the air."

Several students chuckled, and the teacher not only named the apostrophe but proceeded to give four or five more examples of sentences using the mark correctly. The students were somewhat engaged, but what an opportunity this teacher missed to have the students engage in academic discourse. She did what many teachers we see do— she continued to display her own expertise rather than questioning the students and making them do the work.

So what could she have done with her questioning techniques to have improved this part of the lesson? One option would have been to ask students to name the punctuation mark and tell what it is used for; this activity could have been a simple pair-share so that all students were talking about the concept at hand. Then, following the pair-share, she could have modeled a few sentences, some correct and some incorrect, asking the students to describe *why* each was correct or not. This would have forced students to state the rules, such as, "That sentence is correct because Juan is the owner, so the apostrophe comes before the 's' to show ownership." Another option would have been for the teacher to provide a simple definition and engage students in choral response and/or kinesthetic activity to deepen their understanding. After doing something like this, she could have then placed students in groups of three or four and asked them to produce several sentences that displayed the correct use of the apostrophe and possessive pronouns. For example, one sentence with a singular possessive pronoun, one with a plural possessive pronoun, one with an apostrophe for possession, and one with an apostrophe for contraction. This activity could have transpired in five minutes or less and would have been far more engaging for students.

It is imperative that in English language arts lessons, we use our best questioning techniques and all that we know about effective instructional strategies in general so that students are the ones doing the challenging cognitive work, speaking the language of the discipline, and applying their skills.

Using Better Questions with Reading Tasks

Mike Schmoker (2001), not alone in his criticism, has noted that reading instruction often consists of arts and crafts, not authentic reading. He has noted that even Lucy Calkins, a prominent figure in literacy instruction for decades, found a 1 to 15 ratio of reading to "stuff," with student-made dioramas, mobiles, collages, and posters comprising most of that "stuff" (Schmoker, 2009). Schmoker and Graff (2011) have widely promoted the view that argument is the unrivaled key to effective reading, writing, and speaking, and this position is certainly prominent in the Common Core State Standards.

In the early grades, students must learn to decode in order to be capable readers, and much of this early reading instruction includes various forms of practice with identifying letters and sounds. Types of questions used in these early grades focus on the building blocks of learning to read and are therefore often not as broad or challenging as questions that are used in the discussion of literature that is being read aloud to the students and literature students are reading on their own.

There are certain features to keep in mind when using questioning as part of literature discussion, no matter what the age of students. Let's focus on these features now.

Effective class discussions centered on literature engage students fully, help them clarify their learning of many important concepts, and deepen their understanding of the power of literature across time and cultures.

As NCTE (1993) has noted, another force has been at work: "The current era of high-stakes testing has resulted in a narrowed curriculum in many schools, leaving little time or resources for extended interaction with literature."

Unlike the past generation of state standards, the Common Core calls for teachers to use complex texts with students at all grade levels and for these texts to be the focus of much of the instruction in English language arts lessons and classes. Because one of the main goals for college and career readiness is for students to read complex text independently and proficiently—and to communicate their understanding of such texts in speaking and writing—teachers need to build in significant time for the shared reading and discussion of quality literature as a whole class so that students are well prepared to meet the challenges ahead.

Debra Peterson and Barbara Taylor (2012) suggest a sequence in which teachers pose good questions about a shared text, model a response, have students write, convene small groups for discussion of the questions, and ask probing questions of the groups.

The teachers studied by Peterson and Taylor did the following to change their questioning techniques so that they were using more thought-provoking questions:

- Teachers worked in grade-level team meetings to compare how students were doing and to share higher-order questions they were writing (and that their students wrote or were asking).

- Teachers met in cross-grade groups to go deeper by reading, researching, reflecting, etc. They even used videos of their students taking part in the literature discussions to aid in their study.

- Teachers worked with literacy coaches during this process.

Students in the classrooms of the teachers using this rich action-research process grew more in reading achievement than students who did not have these teachers.

The actions described above apply to whole-class reading instruction; what about another typical structure used in reading instruction—the guided reading group?

Nancy Frey and Douglas Fisher (2010) say that small-group guided instruction is perhaps the most complex type of teaching. Indeed, at its best, guided reading instruction of small groups includes the teacher closely watching each individual, continually monitoring how the instruction is going, and gradually pushing each student toward greater independence.

Fisher and Frey (2010) found that the most effective guided reading teachers used the following types of questions:

- Elicitation—asking students to give information or deal with a misconception

- Elaboration—asking students to tell more about something they said or to find evidence in the text; usually following an elicitation question

- Clarification—digging deeper into students' content knowledge; also often used after elicitation questions

- Divergent—asking students to draw on background knowledge or put various aspects of conceptual knowledge together. For example, "Why might the Sierra Nevada mountain range be called 'the backbone of the state'?"

- Heuristic—asking students to state a rule, technique, or strategy

- Inventive—inviting students to create or speculate; for example, asking students to make a list of items that would be vital for an astronaut traveling to Mars

Perhaps what we can be most conscious of during small-group instruction is all the types of questions we could ask. As Fisher and Frey document, there are many, many questions possible. The trick is to plan for these varieties and to remember to not just use the elicitation and elaboration questions that come so readily to our minds.

And, we should not forget the power of having students create their own questions about reading material. Actively processing text to form questions has been shown to yield a 23 percentile-point gain on standardized reading tests (Alliance for Excellent Education, 2011).

Using Better Questions with Writing Tasks

In teaching writing, there are two primary modes in which teachers work: the whole-class lesson, and conferences, which include either one writer or sometimes multiple writers who have similar instructional needs. Effective questioning is perhaps most critical in the small-group or individual conferences. As teacher and author Kelly Gallagher (n.d.) often says, "Remember that you can achieve more in a two-minute conference than you can by spending five to seven minutes writing comments on a paper."

As we have discussed in other sections of this book, questioning in whole-class lessons is very important, but since much of the best instruction in the art of written expression occurs in conference situations, let's focus there for now. These conferences have been at the core of the writing workshop model of instruction, along with mini-lessons directed to the entire class, as far back as the early 1980s when first promoted widely by Donald Graves (1982) and later popularized by Lucy Calkins and Nancie Atwell, among other authors in the field of effective literacy instruction.

Specific, detailed feedback is key in a writing conference. As John Hattie (2012) notes, the best feedback, from the learner's perspective, seems "just in time and just for me." But because writing sometimes inspires anxiety in students, encouragement is also key.

Angela has used these guiding questions successfully for years with high school writers. They are used in both peer conferences and in conferences Angela has with individual students or small groups.

- What would you like feedback about? (Posed to the writer)

- What are the strengths of this piece? Name at least one. (Posed to the person giving feedback)

- What do you have questions about? (Could be from either perspective—writer or person giving feedback)

- What suggestions do you have? Give at least one and be as specific as possible. (Posed to the person giving feedback)

- What will you do next? (Posed to the writer at the end of the conference)

For older students (middle and high school), sometimes just sitting down beside a student and asking, "How's it going with your writing?" is enough to open the conference.

For elementary students, the teacher may have to use more questions and be more specific. Some examples:

- What's happening in your story/piece/composition/report?

- How did you get the idea for your story/piece/composition/report?

- What's your favorite part so far? Why is that your favorite part?

- What would you want someone to remember when they read this?

- Can you tell me more about _____?

- What do you think about this part right here? Does it say everything you want it to say?

- Can you write down what you just said to me? Can I help you do that?

- What will you do next with this piece of writing?

With the implementation of the Common Core State Standards, argumentative writing has come to the forefront of many teachers' minds, particularly secondary teachers, as argumentative writing is called for in all subjects. Effective argumentation will undoubtedly be the focus of many whole-class lessons and assignments in writing.

Schmoker and Graff have summed up the urgency for students to be effective at both written and spoken argumentation:

> "If we want record numbers of students to succeed in post-secondary studies and careers, an ancient, accessible concept needs to be restored to its rightful place at the center of schooling: argument. In its various forms, it includes the ability to analyze and assess our facts and evidence, support our solutions, and defend our interpretations and recommendations with clarity and precision in every subject area. Argument is the primary skill essential to our success as citizens, students, and workers." (2011)

Because written arguments are difficult, students will need many whole-class, small-group, and individual opportunities to craft these arguments. How could a teacher begin? An argument has several parts with which students will need to become familiar, but we should heed George Hillocks (2010): "Perhaps they will learn the terms, but I am quite certain they will not learn to develop strong arguments on their own. To learn that, they will have to become engaged in a highly interesting activity that is both simple and challenging, for which feedback is immediate and clear, that allows for success and inspires further effort...."

Hillocks engages his students in argument first by presenting a picture depicting a murder scene. Immediately the students are engaged, looking for clues that will help solve the crime. He leads them in questioning and clarifying their thinking as they examine the evidence in the picture.

• What do you think?

• Why do you think that?

• Do the rest of you agree with that?

• Is _____ consistent with _____?

• Is _____ important? Why or why not?

These general questions can be used to decipher another's argument and also when crafting one's own.

Using Better Questions with Speaking and Listening Tasks

Students should get plenty of practice in speaking and listening in our classrooms, but the evidence is much to the contrary. As far back as the 1980s, true discussion was found in as little as 4 percent of class time (Goodlad, 1984). More recent studies (Pianta, Belsky, Houts, and Morrison, 2007; and a 2004 study by Learning 24-7) have not indicated substantial change. It is absolutely imperative that educators address this crisis of silence immediately.

The Common Core standards address this lack of student talk with the speaking and listening standards, which are significantly different from most state standards in this area. The most striking difference is in the standards that call for students not only to participate in various forms of classroom conversation but also to *initiate* discussions and to *come prepared* to contribute to discussions. These expectations make it clear that students must be actively involved not only in engaging in academic discourse once the teacher sets the parameters for it, but also bear responsibility for generating discourse.

"Community circle" (Gibbs, 1987) is an effective strategy to use in any classroom so that students can become comfortable with increased speaking and listening demands. The agreements for conducting oneself in a community circle discussion are as follows, according to Gibbs:

- Listen attentively. (In Angela's experience, students will need a great deal of modeling and guidance to do this.)

- Show appreciation and don't use put-downs. You may want to remind students that "put-downs" also include those of oneself.

- Exercise the right to pass if you don't have anything to say when it's your turn. The person facilitating the circle comes back to all who passed to see if they want to chime in before the discussion ends.

- Show mutual respect. This means listening with your eyes, ears, and heart—paying full attention to those speaking, and being conscious of body language (like sighing, eye rolling, etc.).

Usually, teachers start the community circle with a prompt or question and then either choose someone to start or allow someone to volunteer. It's important for the teachers to give students more daily practice speaking. And students must listen to their peers, not just to the teacher.

Another important function of classroom discourse is the application of general and subject-area vocabulary. Students are often listening to teachers drone on and on, supplying all of the important words instead of pulling those words from the mouths of the students. With very young students, obviously, meaningful talk is necessary not only for academic discourse but also to enhance reading. As stated in Appendix A of the English language arts Common Core State Standards (National Governors Association Center for Best Practices and Council of Chief State School Officers, 2010, p. 26), "If literacy levels are to improve, the aims of the English language arts classroom, especially in the earliest grades, must include oral language in a purposeful, systematic way, in part because it helps students master the printed word." Students learn new vocabulary only with repeated use of and exposure to the words. Classroom discussion must help them have multiple opportunities to read, write, say, and listen to general words they don't yet know and the most important words in the discipline.

Conducting Socratic discussion, or formal Socratic seminars, is another way to help students improve their speaking and listening skills. However, these discussions can't just be implemented on a whim; they must occur in a carefully cultivated learning environment and must be planned very carefully.

When operating well, however, Socratic discussions allow students to take the lead and to direct classroom conversation instead of being continually led by the teacher. In Matt Copeland's book *Socratic Circles* (2005), he shares the excerpt of Socratic discussion below. Notice how the students respond to each other and take the conversation in different directions as they discuss the poem "Beating Time" by Barbara Kingsolver:

Brittany: Obviously she's upset that Arizona got rid of poetry...

Jimmy: What makes you say that?

Brittany: Look at the lines and the way she worded things . . . "interdicted, evicted, squanders." It's like she's screaming at the governor.

Stephanie: I agree . . . She's trying to convince others she's right so that maybe people will realize their mistake before it's too late.

Tyler: Too late for what?

Stephanie: Too late for poetry . . . It's like a whole art form would be lost forever.

Jimmy: It's not like poetry is difficult . . . People could still figure it out even if it wasn't taught in school. I don't understand what she's so mad about.

Jose: You're probably right. People probably would still be able to figure out poetry, but I'm not sure they would figure it out as well ... I mean, every time I read a new poem, it gets easier, and what I learn in one poem I can usually use in another poem.

Stephanie: You lost me.

Jose: In the middle of the poem, she says, "where the fans overhead / whispered 'I am, I am' in iambic pentameter." If it wasn't for studying poetry in school, I'd have no idea what iambic pentameter was.

Brittany: Yeah ... The more you learn about something, the more you are going to understand it.

Jose: I think it's more than that, though. I think that's her whole point.

Stephanie: What's her whole point?

Jose: She's saying if poetry isn't taught in school, if we don't learn about all the ... devices poets use, then we ... won't understand all the poetry that's going on all around us all the time.

Brittany: We become like poetry morons who don't understand or appreciate the beauty of poetry ... Then she has no one to communicate with, no one to share what she writes with, and we all just sit there dumb. That's what she's angry about.

Jose: Exactly.

The students in Matt Copeland's classroom have obviously learned how to go into a text repeatedly, connect an author's ideas to their own life experiences, challenge each other, and present their varied points of view to each other in a respectful way. These are all aims of Socratic discourse.

The vignette on Socratic discussion that appears prior to this chapter exhibits several powerful truths about quality literature discussion. First, it does not unfold naturally or quickly, but with patience and effective prompting, it will happen. It may not happen the way the teacher had envisioned, or as quickly as desired, but it will occur. Second, the teacher must recast his or her role from leader to participant. Socratic discussions are built upon provocative questions, which at first the teacher needs to plan. However, as students become more comfortable with the format, they will create questions that they can open the discussion with, and they will create many wonderful questions as they explore the shared text. Last, the time is worth it. Deep discussion takes time—but it also "sticks with" those who engaged in it. Slow down, develop more powerful questions, and let the conversation unfold.

Scenarios of Effective Questioning in Action

Principal Majalise Tolan shares this example:

> The most effective (and my favorite) assessment ever was in a world literature class after we read *Jane Eyre*, by Charlotte Bronte. We had been working on formulating strong questions throughout the unit and had closely examined characterization, theme, and author's purpose.
>
> Students all drew the name of a character from a bag. That night they reviewed the text and notes we had taken to better study their primary character. The next day in class, they were given five other character names and had two days to study relationships among all those characters and to develop questions. Those questions were turned in to me, scored, and then given to students representing those primary characters. Those students answered the student-created questions as homework. The next day, the students had a "tea party" (I did let them dress up and drink tea for fun—the boys were adorable with their

moms' teacups). The students had their questions and went and had a conversation with the other students whom they asked and answered questions of. I walked around the room and listened and watched for social behaviors (good volume, eye contact, comfortable distance from the person they were talking to, etc.). The students were assessed based on their written responses, but they also got valuable practice speaking about their characters knowledgeably.

I used this format again the next year, but we mingled with the AP students across the hall, who also read *Jane Eyre*. My world literature students were better than the AP students at formulating questions that elicited strong responses.

This scenario exemplifies the power of student-created questions. Once students experience powerful questioning as a normal part of their learning environment, then they are well equipped for engaging in this type of student-to-student questioning. And, truly, isn't that much more authentic? Students questioning each other about literature they've read is more like what happens in the world outside school when people discuss their current reading.

Master teacher Leanne Geary shares these powerful questions that were used in a guided reading group discussion in a 5th-grade classroom. The students were reading the book *Pictures of Hollis Woods*, by Patricia Reilly Giff. Notice how the questions nicely align with the Common Core reading standards that require students to focus on the interactions among literary elements and to examine how ideas and characters develop throughout the course of a text.

• Based on what we know about Hollis, what predictions do you have about her new foster home placement?

- What might make her change her initial reaction to Josie?
- As Hollis learns more from and about Josie, how do Hollis's feelings change?
- How does Patricia Reilly Giff describe Hollis in the beginning of the book?
- How does Hollis's character change throughout the book?
- How does the author use art and photography to portray change in Hollis?
- What other characters change because of their interactions with another character in the book?
- What are the key events in the plot that lead to Hollis changing?
- If the book ended in another way, how would you want it to end?

Guided reading groups, if well managed, can help students develop confidence in their own questioning techniques and in engaging in academic discourse with their peers. However, they can also turn into the "ping pong" game where the teacher "pings" a question to one student, gets the "pong" of an answer, and then continues to "ping" questions at the other students. When guided reading works best, it is more of an authentic discussion in which the teacher takes the lead—but does not have to keep the lead. It's a perfect setting, with literature at the "just right" reading level for students in the group, for them to learn to take increasing responsibility for questioning, probing, reflecting, and speaking with confidence about literature.

When working with students on their writing, individual and small-group conferences are key. Below are examples of each.

Individual Conference

The teacher walks over to a student who is working on his writing in the writing workshop portion of class.

Teacher: Are you able to take a break from drafting and talk with me about your work?

Student: Sure.

T: Tell me how it's going so far. Remind me of your topic.

S: I'm writing about the lasting effects of the Civil Rights movement. About how the progress made didn't just help blacks, but also helped other minorities, and women, too.

T: That's right. I remember I gave you the go-ahead on your thesis statement and your plan a couple of days ago. Is it coming along smoothly?

S: I need some more information for the paragraph on other minorities being helped. I have a body paragraph about the rights that blacks gained, and I have lots of information about how the movement helped women, especially in the workplace. But my information on the other minorities seems like it's not enough.

T: What do you mean "not enough"?

S: Well, I don't have many details in that paragraph.

T: (Reads the paragraph.) Well, what about including religion in addition to race? Have you thought about that? How would that change your paper?

S: Oh yeah, like Jewish people were discriminated against and couldn't even vote in some states before this.

T: There you go! Now you're onto something. See what you can find out about racial, religious, and gender discrimination.

(End of conference.)

Small-Group Conference

Teacher: Thanks for coming over here to meet with me. I know you're all working very hard on your essays. Let's talk about where each one of you stands. Who would like to start?

Student 1: I will. I've got my plan for writing and I've written my introduction paragraph. That's about it so far. I know what I'm putting in the body but I've just gotta write that part.

T: Great! Sounds like you're making progress and know just where you're heading. How long will your body be?

S1: I'm thinking four paragraphs. I have four pretty solid reasons supporting my claim, so that's where I'm headed.

T: Good. When you get into it, let me know if I can help. Who's next?

Student 2: I'm a little farther than that. I'm in the body part. I have four body paragraphs too, and I'm working on the second one now.

T: Thanks! Maybe we can all get back together when each of you has the body completely drafted. What about you?

Student 3: I have an introduction and a plan for the body, but I went ahead and wrote my conclusion paragraph. I hope that's okay. Then I'm gonna go back and do all the body parts.

T: That's a terrific idea, writing the beginning and then the end, if that works for you. So now you just have to do the middle, right? It's like you're making a sandwich, and you have the two pieces of bread to hold it together, and now you've got to create the fillings. Or like bookends on a shelf. You've got placeholders. You just need to put the between stuff in.

S3: Yeah, it's kinda like a sandwich right now. But I wanted my intro and conclusion to match up tight, so that's what I did.

S1: I might try to write my conclusion and then go back to do the body of the essay. I was feeling kinda bored or stuck after I wrote the intro and now I'm not so excited about the middle. So doing it that way might free up my mind a little, to go to the end.

T: Good strategy. Try it and see what you think. There's no one perfect way to do this.

S2: I think I'll just keep going and then do the conclusion last. But next time I might try something different, especially if I get bored or I feel stuck.

T: All right, everyone. I think you're all in good places. The three of you may even want to get together later in class today, once you all have drafts of a conclusion, just to bounce ideas off each other. Also, would you each think about how you're moving the reader from body paragraph to body paragraph? Remember how we looked at those transition ideas? Be sure you think about how to use them, and of course, talk to each other about this if you like.

(End of conference.)

Another important use of questioning is to help students become more metacognitive. Reflecting on one's writing *in writing* can help students improve their writing significantly over time and can also help students become better assessors of their own work. The handout in Figure 3.1 was used successfully for several years in high school English classes.

FIGURE 3.1   **Student Handout—Reflecting on Writing**

Final Draft Reflection Sheet

Please answer each of the following in complete sentences in the spaces provided. Attach this sheet to the back of each final draft you submit. Papers submitted without this sheet *will not be graded.*

1. As the writer of this piece, are you satisfied with it? Why or why not? Explain. If you're not satisfied, explain what you would like to do next with it.

2. What do the title and beginning/lead of this piece do to engage the reader and make him want to keep reading? Explain.

3. How did you make sure that you have correct form/structure, mechanics, and grammar?

4. Who is the intended audience for this piece?

5. What is your favorite line, sentence, example, or detail in this piece? Why is that one your favorite?

6. Name all the people that helped you with your drafts. (Do not include your teacher.) Share one helpful thing you remember from each person.

7. Use the back of this sheet for a full explanation, if more space is needed. Based on the rubric that applies to this piece of writing, what grade do you deserve? Why? (Your teacher will write back to you about your grade.)

VIGNETTE
A REFLECTION ON QUESTIONING
By an Instructional Coach

My role has led me to observe all kinds of practices and both effective and ineffective teaching strategies. A strategy that teachers felt particularly focused on this past year in my district was questioning. A few teachers that I worked with and observed developed some great insight with questioning and worked to perfect questioning during instruction.

What I have come to realize and have relayed to others is that questioning involves much more than just the questions that are posed to the students and the responses to those questions. Questioning involves wait time, carefully planned questions that relate to the content, randomly calling on students, the use of nonnegotiables, ... and the list could go on.

Three particular situations really stand out where teachers had "a-ha" moments about their use of questioning in their classrooms.

Early in the school year, I observed a 2nd-grade teacher. She had asked me to observe, collect data, and provide feedback on teaching to the daily learning target. As I observed, I wrote down everything the teacher said and everything I observed during her science lesson. I did my best to be a true transcriber of all that was happening.

Later in our post-observation conference, I presented her with information about her lesson, asking her to share how she thought she did with teaching to the target. One of her definite strengths was how all of her activities were aligned with her target. However, I asked her to look at the questioning from her lesson. I had highlighted all of the questions she had posed. I asked her what she noticed about them. She accurately noted that she had asked a lot of questions throughout the lesson. I then asked her to look at the content of her questioning and tell me what she noticed.

By examining her own questions, she had realized that *all* of her questions were behavioral or procedural questions. Not a single one of her questions throughout her lesson had to do with the content she was teaching or with her objective! Her questioning included:

"Are you supposed to be doing that?"

"Where are you supposed to be sitting?"

"Where do your hands go?"

"What are the steps that we follow?"

These questions led her away from the content and did not help to engage the students in the lesson or the learning.

Our discussion helped her to really focus on her questioning and the content of her questions. I suggested she prepare some questions prior to teaching her lesson that would be focused on the content and the learning targets for the lesson. I suggested posting the questions at the beginning of the lesson to help guide her and stay focused.

Another teacher I observed, this one in first grade, had asked me specifically to collect data on his use of questioning during a math lesson. This teacher came to realize he had not asked any questions at all in a 30-minute lesson. Even during the independent practice session, he would give students hints and other cues, but he didn't pose one single question. This was shocking to both him and me.

Yet another teacher, this one of third grade, asked me to collect data on his use of questioning. He had been working on phrasing his questions all year and wanted to pose more higher-level questions during instruction. I observed a math lesson and recorded all of the questions.

When we analyzed his questions, we came to the conclusion that many of his questions revolved around what the students found to be interesting rather than what was important to the content. This is one of the main cautions in *Classroom Instruction That Works* (Marzano, Pickering, and Pollock, 2001) and other respected professional books—don't get sidetracked and pay more attention to the unimportant parts of the content—stick to what's most important.

All of these situations really opened these teachers' eyes to questioning and how powerful it really can be when strategically planned. As these teachers became focused on their questioning, they noticed increased student engagement and improved learning outcomes.

CHAPTER 4

Powerful Questioning in Mathematics

‿oc

"In mathematics the art of proposing a question must be held of higher value than solving it."
Georg Cantor

We begin this chapter with a reflection from Deb Moore, a mathematics teacher and instructional coach and one of the three authors of this book:

> I was not a strong math student in middle and high school, with my struggles beginning when I was introduced to x, y, and the coordinate plane. What did those letters mean? Why was I plotting these points on a coordinate plane, and how did it relate to the equations? Even worse, how did I work with those equations to generate my own x, y pairs, and why bother?
>
> It wasn't until my second year of college that math really began to make sense. Believe it or not, it was in my elementary mathematics methods course that my transformation began. My instructor, Sr. Armella, was frustrating at first; we would ask questions, she would respond with more questions … back and forth, never giving the answers to any of us. I very quickly realized that as a result of this questioning, my conceptual understandings about

the basics of math were challenged and then reshaped as a result of the dialogue … the "whys" behind all of the algorithms I'd learned throughout school were finally understood. As a result of my newfound proficiency in an area I once hated, I wanted to know more and I wanted to share what I'd learned. Why didn't all teachers lead us to the "whys"?

I went on to earn my undergraduate degree in education (conferred with honors) and a minor in mathematics. I am a teacher of mathematics at the secondary level—grade 6 mathematics through honors geometry—and I am currently an instructional resource teacher and coach specializing in mathematics.

What happened? It wasn't until about my fifth year of teaching that it clicked … "Mrs. Moore, it is so frustrating! Just tell me how to do it!" It was an "a-ha" moment as I realized I was doing what frustrated me at one time—answering a question with more questions or having students discover a formula or algorithm on their own before officially defining it. I can still picture Michael, sitting in one of my algebra sections, blurting this out as I led the class to discover the formula for calculating the next term of a geometric sequence.

Of course I did not tell him the answer, and he did discover the formula by the end of the lesson. He now had something that he could draw from if, as he most likely did, he forgot the formula in some later math course or on the ACT. Indeed, instilling this conceptual knowledge is steeped in both the practice and content standards as defined by the new mathematics Common Core State Standards. "Students who lack understanding of a topic may rely on procedures too heavily ... In short, a lack of understanding effectively prevents a student from engaging in the mathematical practices" (National Governors Association Center for Best Practices and Council of Chief State School Officers, 2010).

In my own learning and practice, I've come to discover that asking powerful questions can be one of the most effective ways to bridge both the practice and content standards. This is where, I believe, the waters become muddied when determining whether teaching is a science or an art; to really listen to students and to have such a deep conceptual knowledge of the content so as to be able to respond and continue to question and probe is really a delicate balance of both art and science.

What do powerful questions look like in mathematics? What does a classroom look like that engages in questioning and dialogue as a primary means of leading students to discover on their own? In this era of accountability and testing, it is more important than ever that math educators continue to focus on inquiry, not just for the sake of preparing for the tests, but also to provide students with the content and practice needed for them to become fully engaged in mathematics, even if it takes them until college to get there.

Background

There has been much research conducted on the impact that asking powerful questions in the classroom has on student achievement. There is not, however, much statistical data that directly correlates the use of powerful questions to an increase in student achievement in mathematics. But there is enough research on what *does* have a powerful impact on mathematics achievement to be able to come to the

conclusion that asking powerful questions in the mathematics classroom does, indeed, increase achievement.

The eight mathematical practices outlined in the mathematics
Common Core State Standards (CCSS) are processes and proficiencies
that have long been recognized as being important components of
mathematics education. Embedded within the standards and explic-
itly stated is the need for students to be able to "construct a viable argument," justify an explanation or answer, and aptly "critique the
reasoning of others" (National Governor's Association Center for Best
Practices and Council of Chief State School Officers, 2010). This type
of discourse does not occur naturally in a classroom setting; the behaviors needed for this type of discourse must be modeled, and students must be invited to become active participants in the process. As
teachers, we've done a good job of asking students to explain their answers, but our questions need to go beyond that. Currently, the solution to a problem, or an explanation about how the solution was
obtained, accounts for much of the discourse within the "school
mathematics tradition" (Voigt, 1995). We ask our students a question
with some idea as to how we would like them to respond. Students,
in turn, attempt to "guess" what it is we want to hear and respond ac-
cordingly. We evaluate the answers we receive, moving on from student to student until we find the answer we are looking for. This is
not a criticism, but rather an observation and an opportunity to reflect upon and improve our practice.

In what Voigt distinguishes as the "inquiry mathematics tradition" (1995, p. 198), student explanations are only the beginning, as
they are what drive the discourse in classrooms where students are
encouraged to engage in the mathematical practices as outlined in the
Common Core. Rather than ending a discussion by providing the
right or expected answer, students' responses become the focus of the
discussions. For this to occur, "a teacher must be skillful at posing

questions that challenge student thinking, listening carefully to students' ideas, rephrasing students' explanations in terms that are mathematically more sophisticated, deciding when to provide information, and orchestrating class discussions to ensure participation by all students" (Peressini, Borko, Romagnano, Knuth, and Willis, 2004, p. 79).

Elementary Mathematics: Place Value and Base Ten

While counting and cardinality are highlighted in the Common Core, they are relegated to kindergarten only. The new standards call for an emphasis on number, algebraic thinking, geometry, operations, and operations in base ten in the elementary grades 1–5. Numbers and operations with fractions are introduced and mastered in grades 3–5. These emphases are not necessarily new, but the conceptual understandings that students are expected to have developed with regard to these topics have deepened considerably and are essential for success in mathematics at higher grade levels.

In particular, emphasis has been placed on developing an understanding of place value and base ten; both are critical concepts that are necessary precursors for success in working with operations in base ten in grades 1–5 as well as decimals and percentages in the middle school years. These are areas that students tend to do more poorly in on standardized tests. What types of questions can we use to initiate the type of discourse in our elementary classrooms that research has shown us to be most effective?

> A group of five students sat closely around the teacher on the carpet in the first-grade classroom. The sounds of laughter, bouncing rubber balls, and children's voices carried in through the open windows. It was recess, but these students elected to stay behind to work a bit more on the

math concepts covered in the lesson earlier in the day. The topic: adding a two-digit number and a one-digit number.

Teacher: Okay, so let's take a look at a problem from our lesson today. How about 12 + 9?

CJ: It's 21.

T: How did you know that so quickly, CJ?

CJ: Nine is one away from ten, and I already have one ten. So, I took one from the two extra in 12 and added it to the 9. Now I have two tens and one left over.

Allie: I got 12, but I know that's not right, because I started with 12.

T: How did you get 12? Could you explain it to us?

Allie: Now I got 21 by counting. When I add 2 + 9 I get 11, and then I add the one extra for 12.

The above scenario is one that plays out in classrooms everywhere. Allie clearly has a procedural understanding of how to add single-digit numbers, and she is having difficulty working with the addition of two-digit numbers and one-digit numbers. But is her difficulty the result of a lack of understanding of base ten, or is it a lack of number sense?

Before we can successfully craft questions to initiate and facilitate meaningful discourse in our classrooms, we need to first ask ourselves questions about potential difficulties that students might have. We must be careful, though, not to be too quick to provide answers to those questions—our work should instead focus on developing questions to get students thinking, so that they can form their own understandings. What types of questions could be used to determine whether Allie struggles with number sense or if she really doesn't understand base ten? And what types of questions could then be posed to Allie and to the rest of the class to begin the discourse that will engage the students in the mathematical practices outlined in the Common Core?

T: Allie, why did you add the extra one?

Allie: I don't know ... it can't just stay there.

T: Can you show me what 12 looks like?

Allie grabs a stack of cubes and begins counting until she has 12 in front of her.

T: Is there another way to show 12?

CJ: She should group them into a ten with two left.

Allie: I'm going to do six and six.

CJ: But then you can't add.

Allie appears to be confused, frowning at the cubes before her.

Allie: But, 6 + 6 is 12!

T: CJ, what do you mean by that?

CJ: If we have one stack of ten and two left over that is like writing 12.

T: Could you go to the board to show us using the cubes and numbers how to write "12" using the cubes?

CJ takes the cubes and walks to the chalkboard. He places the stack of ten to the left of the two extra on the chalk tray, picks up a piece of chalk, and writes a "1" above the stack of ten and a "2" above the two extra.

CJ: See? The numbers I wrote make 12, which is one "ten" group and two "ones" left.

T: So, is that what you meant when you said you already have one group of ten?

CJ nods as he walks back to join the group.

T: How did you then add the 9 so quickly? Can you show us with the cubes?

CJ carefully counts out nine more cubes and heads to the board.

CJ: I have nine ones and need one more to make a ten group. (He clicks eight cubes together and adds the two extra cubes on the chalk tray to make a second group of ten.)

Two ten groups and one left over is 21.

Allie: Oh! I forgot that the one was a ten group. Shouldn't you move the new ten group next to the other one?

T: Why do you say that Allie? Can you show us what you mean?

Allie walks to board.

Allie: Now I have two ten groups and one left over.

She erases the "1" and "2" that CJ drew on the board earlier.

Allie: We have two ten groups and one left over—21.

When reading through the preceding vignette, notice that the teacher never gave the students a direct answer. Rather, she guided them toward their own understandings by asking pointed questions that would take them there. Also note that prior to this event, the children had been working extensively with cubes to establish number and work on the idea of place value. Not only is the teacher modeling the Common Core's standards for mathematical practice for her students, they are also meeting a number of the standards as outlined in the domain "numbers and operations in base ten" for grade 1.

In the next vignette, we visit a 2nd-grade classroom where students are beginning to expand their understanding of place value and base ten by exploring three-digit numbers, a concept important for the upcoming work in grades 3 and 4 in the areas of using place value understanding to perform multidigit arithmetic. We are observing only the opening of the lesson as it illustrates how questioning can make explicit the concepts we want our students to engage in so as to make connections and to develop deep conceptual understandings.

Bags of math money consisting of pennies, dimes, and dollar

bills are placed on each group's table, along with a place value mat and an accompanying activity worksheet with three columns drawn on it to represent hundreds, tens, and ones. The students enter the room after music class, notice the manipulatives on their tables, and quickly go to their seats.

The teacher is standing in the front of the room with a precariously balanced stack of 100 pennies and a smaller stack of 10 pennies next to it on the table in front of him.

"Be careful not to bump my table, please. It took me a long time to carefully build my tower of pennies," he cautions the students.

"Mr. Harris, why do you have that big tower of pennies?"

"How many are there?"

"Do we get to build a tower?"

The questions erupt from a number of students, their interest clearly piqued. A few children open the bags and begin to construct their own towers; Mr. Harris allows them a few minutes to play with the manipulatives. One student from group four notices the dollar bills in the bag and asks, "How many pennies do you have in the big tower?"

Mr. Harris uses this question to focus attention back to the front of the room.

"We have a very good question here from Caleb. Would you like to share your question with everyone?"

"I asked how many pennies were in the big tower on the table."

"Caleb, why did you ask that?" asks Mr. Harris. A few other children raise their hands as well.

"If you have 100 pennies in your tower, why didn't you use a dollar bill?"

"Hmmm ... I do have 100 pennies in the taller tower."

A few heads begin to nod, and it is evident that one little girl in group three is starting to make a connection as evidenced by her reaction to Caleb's statement and Mr. Harris's confirmation that there are, indeed, 100 pennies in the taller tower. Mr. Harris notices this as well and asks the following: "Why would Caleb say that I could use a dollar bill instead of stacking 100 pennies? Emma, would you like to share?"

Emma, the girl in group three who clearly reacted to Caleb's question, answers, "Because there are 100 pennies in a dollar."

"I bet the smaller tower has 10 pennies in it!" calls out another student.

"Let's count them out and see," replies Mr. Harris, who begins counting. The class joins in after he counts out the second penny.

"... 3, 4, 5, 6, 7, 8, 9, 10!"

"Andrew, why did you guess that the smaller tower is made up of 10 pennies?"

"Because you had 100 pennies in the big tower and we have dollar bills in our group and dimes in our group. Ten pennies is one dime."

"Oh! And 10 dimes is one dollar bill!" comments a second student in Andrew's group. Mr. Harris wants the students to focus on the relationships between and among pennies, dimes, and dollar bills, and uses the following questions to elicit students' understandings prior to starting the lesson.

- What's the relationship between pennies and dimes? Between dimes and dollar bills?

- How does the relationship between pennies and dimes compare with the relationship between dimes and dollar bills?
- Why do we use one dime to represent 10 pennies or one dollar bill to represent 100 pennies?

"Let's use our place value mats to look at different ways to represent how much money we have. How can we model 123 cents? Work in your groups to model this in as many ways as you can using your money and your place value mat, recording your answers on your activity sheet."

Mr. Harris circulates around the room, working with groups and asking and answering questions. He is careful to make connections between and among all of the different representations students could make. It becomes clear that students understand that we trade 10 pennies for a dime and 10 dimes for a dollar because it is more convenient to carry dollars and dimes than it is to carry 100 or more pennies.

This type of work and the questions used to guide students toward making connections within the work lay the foundation for students' understandings of the standard, "use place value understanding and properties of operations to perform multi-digit arithmetic," found in both grades 3 and 4 in the Common Core.

Making Sense of Fractions, Decimals, and Percentages in the Middle Grades

The previous section focused on ways to use questioning to help students develop deep understandings around the concepts of place value and base ten; fractions, decimals, and percentages are concepts that cannot be mastered without these prior deep understandings. In grade 3, students are expected to "develop understanding of fractions as numbers" and carry this work into grade 4, where they "understand decimal notation for fractions, and compare decimal fractions," and grades 5 and 6, where they are expected to understand and apply operations with fractions and decimals (National Governors Association Center for Best Practices and Council of Chief State School Officers, 2010).

In working with students, I (Deb) have come to expect and plan for extra time spent on covering fractions, decimals, and percentages, as this is an area where many students struggle; many of my colleagues have experienced the same in their classrooms. Students often know how to perform operations with fractions and decimals, but they usually do not understand why they are doing what they do, and if they forget any of the rules, they are stumped. We have a lot of ground to cover, as I often find that I have to go back (almost) to the beginning—I often begin with geoboards and grid paper.

Each student is given a geoboard and a bag of rubber bands. I begin by asking students to use one rubber band to create a four by four square on their board while I model the same on the SMART board.

"Could you now take another rubber band and divide your square in half vertically?" I again model this by moving a rubber band onto my SMART board geoboard and use a color to shade in one of the halves so that it resembles the diagram shown in Figure 4.1.

I ask students to record the name of this fraction in their math journals, and all of them easily name it as 1/2.

"Now take two more rubber bands and divide each half into two smaller halves. How does this new division compare to our first?"

Students are looking at me, not quite sure what I am looking for or thinking that I've somehow lost it during this long stretch we call third quarter. Julia then calls out.

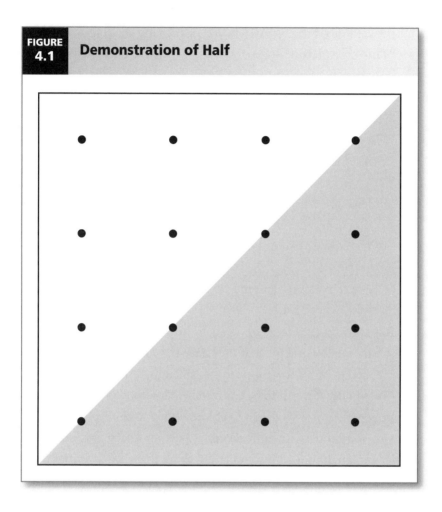

FIGURE 4.1 Demonstration of Half

"We now have four equal parts instead of two."

I model this on the SMART board.

"We have four equal parts, as Julia said. How does the shaded area change?"

"It doesn't change ... half is still shaded."

This is what I was hoping for, as it is a continuation of developing a number sense of fractions in students.

"Are you sure? How do we write 'half' as a fraction?"

"1 over 2."

I write this on the SMART board next to my geoboard.

"This new picture doesn't show 1/2 … I have four equal parts now, not two."

"2/4 is the same thing as 1/2."

"How do you know?"

"They are equivalent fractions because 2/4 reduces to 1/2."

"What does that mean that they are equivalent and 2/4 reduces to 1/2?"

Students are exasperated, not sure why we are taking the time to review something they've already had.

"We can divide two out of both the numerator and the denominator."

"Or, we can take 1/2 and multiply the numerator and the denominator by two to get 2/4."

It is clear that students understand how to make equivalent fractions, but I am looking to see if they have the conceptual understandings needed to move toward proportional and abstract reasoning.

"What does it mean to be equivalent? How would you prove it to a younger student who doesn't yet know how to multiply or divide? Take a few minutes with your shoulder partner to discuss and record a brief explanation for how you could share this with a younger student."

This activity solidified the idea of equivalency for many students as they recognized that the shaded area was a geometric representation of equivalency, making explicit the connection between the concrete and the abstract. Students now had the "why" behind the procedure that they'd learned in earlier grades. It is ideal if students work with the concrete first, but that doesn't always happen. As we begin to work more with the Common Core and recognize the importance of conceptual understandings in addition to procedural knowledge, we will have less and less backtracking to do with our students as we evolve as teachers to reflect these changes in mathematics education.

The resource I relied heavily upon when developing these activities was *Proportional Reasoning* (2003) by Erickson, Anderson, Hillen, and Wiebe, a part of the Algebraic Thinking Series published by the AIMS education foundation. To finish the lesson described above, I use other explorations from the AIMS text that have students modeling and recording other equivalent representations using the geoboard and grid paper. I further developed this concept of number sense of fractions by asking students to determine the whole when given only a part and its fraction name, to determine the fractional value of a visual picture in fraction, decimal, and percent forms, to find the percentage of an identified whole, and to determine the size of a whole when given a picture of the part along with its percentage of the whole to be determined (Erickson, Anderson, Hillen, and Wiebe, 2003).

To further develop the relationships between and among fractions, decimals, and percentages, money is again used in the upper elementary and middle grades, as it directly models the concrete and students are able to abstract from it. Almost all students in these grades are able to write $1.25 and know that it is equal to one dollar and 25 cents, its value if it were used to purchase something. This understanding can serve as an entry point for many students to engage in the work of linking this decimal representation to its value as a percentage and fraction. Quite simply, when using money to represent decimals we use $100 bills to represent hundreds, $10 bills to represent tens, $1 bills to represent ones, dimes to represent tenths, and pennies to represent hundredths. A number of questions could guide the discussion, and an explicit connection between "cent" and "percent" really helps students who are not quite seeing this connection.

- How would you write 45 cents as a decimal?

- How do the numbers of dimes and pennies needed to make 45 cents relate to its decimal equivalent?

- If the $1 bill is our "whole," how could we use this

knowledge to show 45 cents as a fraction? (Some students may need a reminder to break the whole down into 100 cents.)

• What percentage of a dollar is 45 cents? Justify by discussing how the fraction 45/100 represents this.

• How would you write one dollar and 45 cents as a decimal? How would you write 10 dollars and 45 cents as a decimal?

The same line of questioning would be followed for $1.45 and $10.45 to help students to really solidify the concepts of fraction, decimal, and percentage and their relationships to each other. Also, students are once again given the opportunity to reinforce and deepen understandings around place value and base ten.

Grades 7 and 8 really begin to focus on expressions and equations, proportional reasoning, and probability. There are a number of rich mathematical problems that can be used to explore these concepts, but more of the work in middle school should begin to move students toward more abstract, algebraic thinking.

Algebraic Thinking in Middle and High School

While I've used some of the strategies and activities outlined previously in the chapter, developing what Mark Driscoll terms "habits of algebraic thinking" in his book *Fostering Algebraic Thinking: A Guide for Teachers Grades 6–10* (1999) forms the basis for the majority of the work my eighth-grade students and I engage in during a math lesson. Functions, systems, proportional thinking—all are important concepts in secondary mathematics, and I've used Driscoll's habits of mind to explore them. These habits are "doing-undoing" (the ability of students to understand not only how to do mathematical processes but also how to undo them), building rules to represent functions, and abstracting from computation (Driscoll, 1999). He believes that algebraic thinking can be learned and that teachers need to engage in modeling, give purposeful feedback, and "ask a variety of questions aimed at helping students organize their thinking and respond to algebraic prompts" (Driscoll, 1999, p. 3).

The types of problems teachers use to model and to engage students in algebraic thinking need to be rich in mathematical content. The following activities exemplify such problems, and interestingly, many of the preservice teachers I've worked with are familiar with these problems through their college coursework, while many of the practicing teachers I've worked with have never encountered these problems. I am looking at this as an indication that many college teacher education programs are beginning to work with the mathematical education community to instill the mathematical practices and standards outlined in the Common Core State Standards. When reading through the following vignettes and problems, though, it is important to remember it is the explorations of and around the problems and the ensuing discussions that make them exemplary.

Eating Coconuts

A sailor is stranded on a deserted island for one week. During that time he has only coconuts to eat. When he is finally rescued, he has 27 coconuts left. On his first day on the island he was hungry, but he was also exhausted and so he ate only one coconut.

He woke up the next day and was a bit hungrier and so he ate three more coconuts. On day three he ate half of what was left, leaving him with a stomachache, and so he only ate one the following day. A sudden storm blew in that afternoon, depositing 15 more coconuts on the beach. Not knowing how long he'd be there, the sailor gathered them up and added them to his pile. He did not, however, eat any on that fifth day, as he was still sick.

On his last full day on the island he ate 1/10 of the remaining coconuts, and was then rescued in the morning before eating any coconuts on day seven.

How many coconuts did he start with?

This story problem is given to students in a grade 6 classroom on the first day; a greeting written on the board welcomes students and asks them to find their seats and to use the whiteboard under their desks to work through the problem. Students enter the room after being greeted by the teacher at the door, and most find their seats and begin to work on the problem after looking around the room to see who is in the class and if they are sitting near anyone they know— typical first-day behaviors in most classrooms.

It is fairly quiet for the first few minutes after the bell rings, with some students writing furiously and others looking tentatively around, then scribbling a few numbers on their whiteboard after seeing what others are doing. Miss Martin enters the room and, after a few minutes of work time, begins class.

"Any solutions?" she asks as she walks around the room. One student calls out, "54." Miss Martin walks up to the screen and writes the student's solution. "Any others?"

"37!" shouts a boy in the back row.

"No, 36," calls out a third student, a girl in the second row.

Miss Martin records all solutions, and as the list grows, so do the number of volunteers who share their solutions. When the calling out stops, there is a list of 11 solutions on the screen.

"Would anyone like to share how they found their answer?"

One tentative hand eases up in the front left of the room.

"I worked backwards and used pictures to help me."

"Could you explain that a bit more for us?" asks Miss Martin.

"I knew the sailor was stranded for seven days and I knew that he ended up with 27 coconuts when rescued. So I wrote the numbers 1 through 7 on my whiteboard and put '27' under the 7 to show that he had 27 coconuts on the last day."

The teacher models this by recording on the board what she hears the student saying. "Does this look accurate?" she asks him.

"Yeah. To work backwards I then found out how many he had on day six before eating the 1/10 that was in the problem ... he had 30 the day before."

Miss Martin records a "30" under the number six to represent 30 coconuts at the beginning of day six. "Can you tell us how you found 30?"

"One-tenth of 27 is 2.7, but I didn't think we were using parts, and so I rounded it up to three coconuts and added it to 27."

A girl in the second row now raises her hand. "I also worked backwards, but the 1/10 he ate on day six were not 1/10 of day seven." A few more hands shoot up, heads begin to nod.

"Would you like to explain what you mean? I think a few others might have the same idea..."

"The 27 coconuts is what was left after eating 1/10. Ten-tenths is all of the coconuts on day six, and after eating 1/10 there are 9/10 left; the 27 coconuts is the leftover 9/10. That means that on day six he did have 30 coconuts, but we don't need to round, because he did eat three on day six, not 2.7."

The boy who had initially answered the question now calls out, "I got 30, too. What does it matter?"

The teacher sees this as a prime opportunity to uncover what students know and understand about fractions and operations and how these change when working backwards. She does not offer any solutions to the students, but launches into a rich discussion and exploration that lasts into the second day of class.

Many teachers would cringe at the amount of time spent on one problem, especially on the all-important first day of school when processes and procedures are to be explained, but Miss Martin balanced it by wrapping up day one's discussion with the students making a fraction strip of the unit fraction 1/10. Their assignment was to come up with an explanation to satisfy the day's discussion up to this point. She then moved into the necessary first-day routines that begin the school year.

Notice that throughout the discussion the teacher did not offer any solutions nor did she tell students they were wrong. She kept probing, asking them how and why questions. She pushed them further on day two by asking such questions as, "What if on day six he ate 3/10 of the coconuts? What if it were 7/10? How would this change the problem?" It was observed that the teacher restated student responses in a slightly more mathematically sophisticated way and she let student responses guide the discussion and the learning.

Some may wonder what standards this particular problem addresses. Not only does it address several of the mathematical practices in the Common Core, it also provides students with an opportunity to work through the algebraic habit of mind that involves doing and undoing and it gives the teacher a sense of where students are with regard to their understandings of fractions and operations.

Another problem that addresses one of Driscoll's habits of mind involves finding the perimeters of different "trains" created by joining shapes together in succession. The easiest shape to begin with is the equilateral triangle.

The heater hums intermittently in the background as the 7th-grade students begin to move into their math groups. Material handlers, one from each group, go to the front of the room to get a task card from the basket. "If you'd like toothpicks to help with today's work, feel free to take one box for your group from the stack next to the task basket," calls out the teacher as the handlers begin to move toward the front of the room.

Triangle Trains

An equilateral triangle has side lengths of one inch, giving it a perimeter of three inches. If we were to make a train of 50 triangles, what would its perimeter be? Can you write a formula that would predict the perimeter of a train length of "n"? Write down a brief explanation of how you approached and solved this problem. The use of diagrams, tables, and charts to support your work is encouraged.

A murmur of voices fills the room as groups begin to work on their problem.

"This is easy ... the perimeter is 150," states one boy in the first group visited by the teacher.

Almost immediately, another boy in the group interjects, "No way! That's too much!" "Fifty triangles times three does equal 150!" interjects the boy who first answered 150.

"Could you sketch your train for us?" asks the teacher, who has not up until this point said anything. The first boy begins to sketch the train that appears in Figure 4.2.

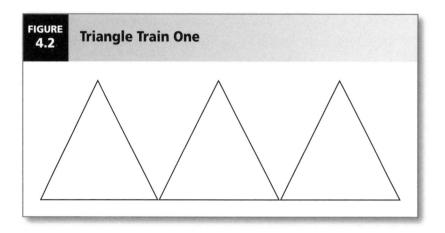

FIGURE 4.2   **Triangle Train One**

"That's not a train," states the second boy.

The only girl in the group sits up a bit straighter and excitedly chimes in, "Oh! I didn't think of a train like that!"

"It is a train," says the first boy at the same time.

The second boy begins sketching out his train, as seen in Figure 4.3.

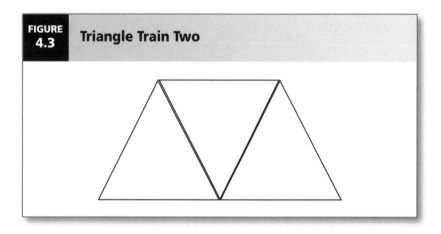

FIGURE 4.3   **Triangle Train Two**

"This is a train!"

The teacher calls out to the class in general, "We have an interesting problem here. What is a triangle train?"

The teacher's prompt leads to a several-minute discussion about what constitutes a train; the class agrees that it is the train shown in figure 4.2. The teacher turns back to the first group.

"This train wouldn't have a perimeter of 150," concedes the first boy. "A lot of sides aren't counted in this train."

"What could your group do to determine what the perimeter is?"

The third boy, silent up until this point, chimes in, "We could make a table and look for a pattern."

"That's a great idea," notes the teacher. "How could you best organize your data so that you could observe any emerging patterns?"

The group eagerly begins discussing how to set up a table and the teacher moves on.

The groups finish their work relatively quickly, all coming to realize that an equation to model this situation could be n + 2, where n equals the number of triangles in the train. Various groups are asked to share their work, and the teacher solidifies the learning by testing out the equation with different numbers of triangles and having the students confirm the results. The teacher extends the lesson by having the students find the perimeters of trains made up of 50 squares, trapezoids, pentagons, and hexagons, again finding an equation that could be used to model each train.

While this is a rich mathematical problem, if it is simply handed to students with minimal explanation and only one approach and one answer is acceptable, then it loses its power. Again, it is the accompanying discussion, driven by the teacher's planned questions along with the students' questions along the way, that really engage the class in constructing viable arguments and critiquing the reasoning of others.

In addition to meeting the Common Core's standards for mathematical practice, this problem is also meeting the grade 7 domain of expressions and equations in the CCSS. In particular, it meets standard 2, "understand that rewriting an expression in different forms in a problem context can shed light on the problem and how the quantities in it are related" (National Governors Association Center for Best Practices and Council of Chief State School Officers, 2010). This standard can be difficult to meet unless teachers are explicit in their instruction by planning for and welcoming questions that allow students to approach a rich problem in a number of ways. In the preceding example, after the students had come up with a list of equations for the different polygon trains, the teacher asked them to note similarities and differences in the equations and posed some of the following questions to guide them in their thinking:

- What's the relationship between Trina's equation for the hexagon train, $4n + 2$ where n equals the number of polygons, and Michael's equation of $(n - 2) + 2$ where n equals the number of sides on each polygon?

- What would the length of a triangle train with a perimeter of 77" be?

- What would the length of a hexagon train with a perimeter of 106" be?

- Compare and contrast the equation for the triangle train with the equation for the square train, rhombus train, pentagon train, and hexagon train.

- What's the relationship between the coefficients of n and the perimeters of the initial polygons used to make the trains?

- How would your equation change if you were to make a train using an equilateral triangle and a square? Choose two polygons and combine them to make a

pattern train of your own; what is the equation that
would model the perimeter of your train?

While an author could devote several books just to exploring the
myriad of problems that are out there to engage students in this type
of discourse and engagement, there is the reality that mandated district
curriculum must be attended to. Many teachers I've worked with
proudly state that they are teachers who do not use the textbook to
teach. I admit, I was there, too. I've come to realize, however, that the
textbook is a great resource that we should use in our teaching. Most
problems, activities, and explorations in textbooks can easily be
changed to reflect the type of work we want to engage our students in.

Peter Sullivan and Pat Lilburn have coauthored a book that focuses on questioning in the math classroom entitled *Good Questions
for Math Teaching: Why Ask Them and What to Ask* (2002). I have referred to this book often in my own teaching and in my coaching work
with other teachers. Although it is primarily geared for kindergarten through grade 6, the concepts are easily adapted to work with
secondary-level mathematics teaching as well.

What is a good question? Sullivan and Lilburn (2002) summarize
it by stating that good questions "require more than remembering a
fact or producing a skill," have more than one acceptable answer, and
are crafted such that students learn in their attempts to answer them
and teachers learn about the students from their attempts (p. 3). They
advocate a three-step approach for creating good questions and offer
two methods for doing so—working backward and adapting a standard question.

As in any good teaching, the first step in both methods is to identify the concept that you want to explore with your students. In the
working backward method they encourage teachers to write an answer
from a closed question and to then make up a question that includes
the answer. In the method that adapts a standard question, teachers

are asked to find a standard question that addresses the concept and rewrite it to make a good question (Sullivan and Lilburn, 2002). I've taken both and reworked the methods so that I have one method that I, and the teachers that I coach, can use when working with our district texts. The process is outlined in Figure 4.4.

FIGURE 4.4   **Process for Creating Good Questions**

Step 1. Identify the concept to be explored.

Step 2. Choose a problem from the text that addresses the concept to be explored.

Step 3. Use the answer given in the text to rewrite the problem, using the answer in the initial question.

One problem that I use in all of my secondary math classes is one that I've adapted using the preceding method. In a typical textbook, students may be asked to find the mean average of a set of scores that students earned on a test (see Figure 4.5). I've taken this problem and instead adapted it so that it is at the somewhat higher level of questioning that involves application (see Figure 4.6).

FIGURE 4.5   **Mean Average Problem**

A student earns the following scores on the five tests given in math class during the first semester: 89 percent, 95 percent, 92 percent, 97 percent, and 98 percent. Calculate the student's mean test average for the entire semester.

FIGURE 4.6 **Higher-Level Mean Average Problem**

A student wants to earn a 94 percent for her mean test average for semester 1 in Mrs. Moore's math class. Her first four test scores are 89 percent, 95 percent, 92 percent, and 97 percent. What must she earn on the fifth test to meet her goal? Be sure to show all of your work, labeling it so that I can follow your process when working through the problem. You may want to use a few sentences or a brief paragraph to further clarify your math work.

To make it a question that involves synthesis and construction, I ask students to find four test scores that could be averaged with a fifth score of 81% for a student to earn an overall mean test average of 94% in my class. They are also asked to explain how they approached the problem, and it is from here that I further ask questions to highlight key concepts or a novel approach that others may not have thought of. This also leads to a great discussion around the importance of practice and study to keep up on the work we engage in.

In this era of accountability and testing it is easy for us to lose sight of the importance of teaching our students to think critically, to engage in discourse, to construct viable arguments, to work well with others . . . all skills that are characteristics of a student who is fully engaged in mathematics, who *is* a mathematician. Our charge as math teachers is to never lose sight of the importance and value of posing good questions to engage our students and ourselves in the logic and beauty that is mathematics.

POWERFUL QUESTIONING
IN SCIENCE AND MATHEMATICS

By an Instructional Coach

In our district there is a shortage of female students in STEM (Science, Technology, Engineering, and Math) classes. For whatever reason, we are not getting enough girls interested in these subjects. After observing the middle school STEM teacher a few times in my role, it was hard to imagine why anyone would not want to be in that class.

Talk about hands-on learning! Students were building and inventing and often did not even realize the magnitude of learning that was taking place. Moreover, the teacher had asked me to work with him on powerful questioning, and after the first observation it was clear that he was a pro at this. I thought he didn't need my help.

STEM is a relatively new program in our district, and like many initiatives in education, it was launched without a lot of time for development and teacher training. The STEM teacher is known for going above and beyond and for being passionate about all his endeavors, though, so he worked hard to make the program one that would be successful.

The teacher confided in me that even though he knew he was effective in questioning, he felt he could improve in this area. He asked me to help him create overarching questions for his STEM units. I thought this was a great idea, as when I first heard that I would be coaching in a STEM class I thought to myself, *what's that?* Using the integrated science, technology, engineering, and math standards to develop a purpose for the learning and designing questions around that purpose to create a framework for learning certainly couldn't hurt.

As we dug through the work he had already done with the standards and looked at the main objectives of the course, one overall purpose became evident: "creating solutions to problems in the world and addressing needs of society." Whoa. That's *huge*. If I were a student in that class and understood that as the purpose of my learning, you had better believe that I would have a reason to figure out how I could apply science, technology, engineering, and math. What's more, I cannot help but think that if the female students in our school district knew that purpose, they would be less hesitant to sign up for STEM. The overall purpose sounded so relevant and exciting.

That teacher and I are working together to create powerful questions for each unit under that one overall purpose that help frame the learning. We are also crafting lesson questions. So, students are experiencing a connected hierarchy of questions. Some examples of unit questions are as follows:

- How does conducting multiple experiments help you prove or disprove a hypothesis?

- How can you help debunk common science misconceptions and inform your local community?

- How does human activity in your neighborhood impact the water quality?

- How would you justify spending federal dollars for more research to improve the medical care or cure rate for a specific disease?

CHAPTER 5

Powerful Questioning in History and Social Studies

∽∘∾

"We learn more by looking for the answer to a question and not finding it than we do from learning the answer itself."

Lloyd Alexander

When a group of social studies teachers gathers for refreshments, the teachers are likely to start discussing what has become a common theme—"Why do all of the interruptions and loss of class time seem to come during social studies?" These teachers believe that social studies is viewed as needing few critical standards and that social studies teachers' time is seen as less critical than in other areas. Why is that? Some may remember only videos and worksheets from their own social studies classes. Others may have had teachers who were efficient and gave their students factual answers to questions they weren't even asking. Dorothy Leeds writes what many think: "All through school, from kindergarten through graduate school, we were encouraged to know the answers, not the questions" (2000, p. 13).

Social studies doesn't consist of merely learning content in history, civics, economics, psychology, and geography; it is the application ground for critical components of the Common Core skills: thinking, reading, and speaking. When social studies curriculum works in balance with instructional strategies, social studies can dynamically connect with students' lives as they gain perspective on conflicts and think creatively to solve real problems.

A good question can be the very match that lights the flame of thinking and learning. It was Albert Einstein who said, "I have no special talent. I am only passionately curious."

In this chapter, we will first look at questions that kindle our curiosity and wonder. "We know that when our curiosity is sparked and we have a desire to know and learn something, our engagement is heightened" (Ritchhart, Church, and Morrison, 2011, p. 13). This launches teachers and students on a learning journey about the concepts at hand. Note that we will use the term "concept" throughout this chapter as Graham Nuthall in *The Hidden Lives of Learners* does, "as shorthand for all the different kinds of knowledge and skills that the teachers want their students to learn" (2007, p. 125). Hopefully, these questions are a catalyst for our students' own questions as natural human curiosity and brain engagement take over.

Secondly, questions clarify what is learned. To that end, John Hattie (2012) contends, "For teachers, questions are often the glue to the flow of the lesson, and they see questions as enabling, keeping students active in the lesson, arousing interest, modeling enquiry, and confirming for the teacher that 'most' of the students are keeping up" (p. 50). There are no clear sequential steps between engagement and clarifying, but it is helpful for us to think about their differences. In this section we include central questions that create quality formative assessment. Black and Wiliam (1998) define this as "encompassing all those activities undertaken by teachers, and/or by their students, which provide information to be used as feedback to modify the teaching and learning activities in which they are engaged."

Now, we know that asking questions is not by itself a formative assessment; we view formative assessment as more fluid, rather than as a product or item to be checked off: "I did my formative assessment on the instructional checklist of today." Instead, we want questions to be intentional—an outcome of interaction with students. As we do this, students begin raising their own questions, which leads to deepening understanding.

A fundamental goal for all learning is to have learners understand the concepts at the level of synthesizing, applying, and evaluating their knowledge, and creating future learning. Deepening understanding becomes visible when facts are not the goal, but are used as building blocks for thinking. "Questions will launch students into areas of study that they would not have approached if their learning were confined to the set of facts distributed through class lectures and materials" (Schell and Fisher, 2007, p. 92). Isn't this our desire as teachers for all learners? The following pages present examples from teachers at the primary, middle, and high school levels. Let these be a springboard for your thinking in your own classes. But before looking at those examples, let's explore an important preliminary use of questions: the Essential Questions around which the unit or lesson is planned.

Essential Questions

Grant Wiggins and Jay McTighe in their work in *Understanding by Design* (2001) highlight the necessity for Essential Questions. They say teachers must choose questions that (Wiggins and McTighe, 2005):

- Are important to argue about
- Are at the heart of the subject
- Recur—and should recur
- Raise more questions, provoking and sustaining engaged inquiry

- Must become habits of mind when we face real problems
- Often raise important conceptual or strategic issues in the subject
- Can provide organizing purpose for meaningful and connected learning

Robert Marzano expands the use of the teacher-generated Essential Questions by adding questions the students create to personalize their goals. In *The Art and Science of Teaching* (2007, p. 179) he says:

"Once students begin to make progress on these goals [teacher-generated essential questions] students are asked to identify their own essential question, so to speak.

"To facilitate students' selection of issues, the teacher might present them with questions such as the following:

- Relative to the content we have been studying, is there an important hypothesis you want to test?
- Relative to the content we have been studying, is there an important decision you want to examine?
- Relative to the content we have been studying is there:
  - An important concept you want to examine?
  - An important past event you want to study?
  - An important hypothetical or future event you want to examine?"

Essential Questions set the frame for a unit or a lesson. Both teacher and students have a clear sense of what "we" are working to learn together. However, that is the teacher's part of the initial process and planning. When the teacher introduces those questions to the class, the real strength comes from students being able to construct meaning and connection to those questions. Teachers are powerful models when using effective questions as a part of the "process" of learning within the unit rather than as "products" to be posted in case a visitor or evaluator stops by. As students create their own goals and questions, the engagement grows. In *Total Participation Techniques*, Himmele and Himmele explain this as the "ripple" of a question (2011, p. 112). A teacher sharing the question or setting a prompt is like someone throwing a pebble in a pond. The power ripples outward through the pond from the initial splash, as does the thinking in the classroom as students reflect and make learning their own.

When students want to discover answers and clearly understand how a task relates to finding the answers, the ripple effect turns into learning and achievement. Dr. Judy Willis, neurologist turned educator, reports on a study with students from the primary grades that makes that connection real in *How Your Child Learns Best* (2008). A class is broken into four groups and given a one-page story to read. Each group is given a different task.

- Group 1: read the story.

- Group 2: read the story, then you will answer questions.

- Group 3: read the story, and be ready to tell the teacher the story.

- Group 4: read the story, and be ready to tell the story to students from a lower grade.

Following their reading, each student is given an identical test. What do you predict the results are? Group 1 scored lowest, and then the scores climbed in order from there. Group 4 scores were the highest. Why? Students knew the task *and* needed to use the reading (Willis, 2008, p. 244). So, what about using Essential Questions could make a strong connection for students?

Making Thinking Visible (Ritchhart, Church, and Morrison, 2011, p. 32) contains a great set of social studies questions. The authors reported finding them on a classroom wall in Washington State. I believe that as soon as the teacher read them to the class both the students and teacher became active learners. The questions:

- What's the story?

- What's the other story?

- How do you know the story?

- Why know/tell the story?

- Where's the power in the story?

Can you visualize these questions in your classroom? They can be adapted for any age. It would be fascinating to follow the increasing depth and richness of the learners' answers as they grow in their thinking and learning. How many times have we been in a classroom and heard the Essential Questions, learning objectives or intentions mentioned in the beginning of the class—never to be heard from again? Every concept we cover in the classroom needs to connect to those questions.

Essential Questions are best when they are a focal point—a touchstone—for students as they move through every lesson and every unit.

Combining the important questions of each lesson with each student's own important questions as they enter class each day would create a powerful catalyst for learning. Students would be drawn to learn each day as they come to school. John Hattie (2012) suggests that pre-lesson questions could include the following (p. 48):

- What are today's goals?

- How much do I already know about today's goal?
  (from "nothing" ... to "a great deal")

- I think today's goal will be ... ("very hard" ... to "very easy")

- How much effort will I put into today's goal? ("none" ... to "a great deal")

Can you envision the student investment one could get if each student declares the answers to these questions? As they personalize their goals, we can make real "inroads" into the content that drives the best of social studies education.

Reviewing the National Council for the Social Studies (1992) definition of the discipline can give us a picture of what that learning could be:

> "Social studies is the integrated study of the social sciences and humanities to promote civic competence. Within the school program, social studies provides coordinated, systematic study drawing upon such disciplines as anthropology, archaeology economics, geography, history, law, philosophy, political science, psychology, religion, and sociology, as well as appropriate content from the humanities, mathematics, and natural sciences. The primary purpose of social studies is to help young people develop the ability to make informed decisions for the public good as citizens of a culturally diverse, democratic society in an interdependent world."

Looking at that definition, it becomes evident that there is some critical work to do with our students for the sake of our collective future.

Once the frame is set with Essential Questions and personalized goals, it's time to look more closely at three areas of focus:

1. Activating prior knowledge

2. Engaging our students

3. Deepening understanding through strengthening literacy

Activate Prior Knowledge

Daniel Willingham has captured the brain-based need for connection to prior knowledge in his book *Why Don't Students Like School?* (2009).

Most people believe that thinking processes are akin to the functions of a calculator. A calculator has available a set of procedures (addition, multiplication, and so on) that can manipulate numbers, and these procedures can be applied to any set of numbers. The data (the numbers) and the operations that manipulate the data are separate. Thus, if you learn a new thinking operation (for example, how to critically analyze historical documents), that operation should be applicable to all historical documents, just as a fancier calculator that does advanced computations can do so for all numbers. However, the human mind does not work that way. When we learn to think critically about, say, the start of the Second World War, that does not necessarily mean we can also think critically about a chess game or about the current situation in the Middle East or even about the start of the American Revolutionary War.

Critical thinking processes are tied to background knowledge (Willingham, 2009, p. 29). We teachers increase our impact when we are aware of the need to transfer skills; our use of questions is key to this process. Our goal is helping students develop thinking and questioning habits. The good news is that the more often we practice these skills together, the easier it is for the students to transfer that ability; and in doing so, they increase confidence in their own capabilities.

Let's look into the 5th-grade classroom of Ms. Lueth. She and her students are beginning to study slavery. Their class goal: to consistently revisit the thinking processes so they learn systems and questions to ask about each scenario of history they cover during the year.

The key year-long goals of social studies for Ms. Lueth are for the students to:

- Understand others' perspectives

- Develop empathy among the students

- Develop the ability to synthesize and integrate content that informs their thinking.

As a framing strategy to introduce this unit, Ms. Lueth asked her students what they would do with the following dilemma: *If you had a choice between wearing ugly boots and having warm feet or wearing cute shoes and having cold feet, what would you do?* Ms. Lueth reminded the students that because people would not have the same view, they were to support others' opinions respectfully and listen respectfully. The class was buzzing about the boot/shoe controversy. When the class is going to move to concepts that may be harder to discuss, it is always a good idea to use a transitional open question as Ms. Lueth did to have the students "warm up their voices" on an opinion question. The class members gain practice being active listeners and respectfully disagreeing with another's opinion. Never underestimate the importance of practice before a class moves on to more intense issues. A well-placed question that the fifth graders could identify with gets the class buzzing and gets the students' brains poised for action. So what about even younger children?

Polly learned a wonderful strategy for activating knowledge in Ms. Cheryl Smith's first-grade classroom in Arizona. Whenever Cheryl asks a question or when her students are learning new words, hearing a story, or having a morning meeting, the classroom is brought to attention as soon as the teacher or students make the motion depicted in Figure 5.1. The entire class stops to listen to the connection that the person has just made. What a great strategy for starting students at a very young age thinking about the power of learning through making connections as they activate their prior knowledge. In Ms. Smith's classroom, if you ask a question, expect that as the answer is coming from one student a connection may be coming from another.

FIGURE 5.1   The Connection Motion

A quick strategy that is used multiple times a week in Polly's advanced placement psychology class is one adapted from Marzano. He calls it "talk a mile a minute" (2007, p. 106), and Polly's classes call it "talk fast."

- Two students work in partnership. (If you have an odd number of students, it will work to have a group of three.)

- Have one person face the screen or front of the room where the paper will be placed. The other person (or two people if there is a group of three) sits with their back(s) to the front of the room.
- First, three to five terms are written on the paper or on a slide presentation, as shown below.

• classical conditioning • unconditioned response • secondary reinforcement • negative reinforcement	

- Without saying the term itself, the student facing the screen gives his or her partner(s) retrieval cues (clues), working on priming the partner's memory until he or she comes up with the term.
- Then students move to the next term, until all four have been completed.
- The partners switch now, and the second list is added.
- The same process is used, with partner 2 giving partner 1 the retrieval cues. Again, if there is a group of three, two stay on the receiving end.

• classical conditioning • unconditioned response • discrimination • negative reinforcement	• operant conditioning • conditioned response • generalization • secondary reinforcement

After everyone completes the task, the class comes back together, and questions become critical.

> Teacher: Does anyone have any questions about these concepts?
>
> Student 1: I don't understand negative reinforcement.
>
> T: Who has insight about negative reinforcement?
>
> Student 2: I have a definition, but don't understand it.
>
> T: We can start there. (S2 reads aloud the definition.)
>
> T: Who can give us insight on clarifying the definition?
>
> Student 3: I think it means punishment.
>
> T: Key insight about the mistake made by the majority of people. Who can give us an example of negative reinforcement?
>
> Student 4: The seat belt buzzer going off in the car, and to get it to stop I put on my seat belt.
>
> T: Now we have an example—who can give us a working definition?
>
> Student 5: That something negative stops.
>
> T: Very helpful. Who has something to add?

The conversation continues until everyone reports a comfort level with the concepts. It is important to go back to the person who first asked for clarification to see if it is indeed clear. After the students have become comfortable with the strategy, it takes about 10 minutes. In turn, both teacher and students gain valuable formative information about the status of learning. Students have often reported that they thought they understood something and then when they tried to come up with the retrieval cues they realized that they needed some additional work to be at the understanding level we strive for in the class.

Engaging the Learner

Do you remember the small child from the first chapter asking, "why?"

When we look at Ms. Van Aalsburg's class of kindergarten students, we see lots of children like that little boy. They were working on friendship. In this lesson, they were observing four large posters. One poster depicts two students coloring with markers, the second shows a pair of students playing with blocks, the third a pair of students playing with balls in the gym, and the fourth a pair of students reading books. The children were asked first what they saw in the pictures. (Remember the bottom-up and top-down processing from Chapter 1?) Students first increase their skills by noting their initial observations. The brain is always looking for patterns and taking in new stimuli. Helping students (especially young ones) practice responding—"What do you see?"—helps them with articulation skills emphasized in the Common Core and also helps teachers know what they are thinking. The questions that bring out students' creativity need to continue throughout school. Sir Ken Robinson portrays students as they progress through school as losing some of their initial wonder and creativity as they reach graduation. Some might even say it was "schooled out of them" as they got better and better at doing school, and less proficient at wondering why and learning. Watch his video on YouTube (http://www.youtube.com/watch?v=zDZFcDGpL4U) ... you'll agree that this is not what we want for students in social studies.

"A student who continues to wonder about different perspectives, missing information, motivations, historic accuracy, ethical considerations, or biases while reading, listening, and thinking about the information encountered in social studies is a student in inquiry mode" (Schell and Fisher, 2007, p. 92). Social studies classrooms can be alive with wonder and engagement.

Let's look into Mr. Josh Bettes' classroom of 5th-grade students in Edina, Minnesota. Their driving question is "Are we there yet?" This is used as a question for engagement, and the students respond with a time they have heard that question while traveling. Taking a look at the trip that Christopher Columbus and others took to come to America, students use that question to incorporate insights from the perspectives of those who traveled with Columbus. To begin their study, they watch a clip on Columbus from Brainpop.com. They use this poem to set the frame:

> You all know the poem 'bout 1492,
> The year that Columbus sailed the ocean blue.
> But where on earth is the rest of the rhyme?
> What else went on 'tween those two short lines?
> You've heard how that sailor left the Spanish shore,
> Taking a route never explored before.
> Still, not much is said of the part of the story,
> Where there's work and there's dirt, and there's little glory.
> Did you know life on the boat was no bed of roses?
> So much to do, no time for dozes!
> Sailors toiled all day and all night,
> Just hoping that land would come into sight.
> In the meantime, they prayed every half-hour,
> And hoped that sea monsters would not them devour.
> Then, when Columbus finally did spot land,
> It wasn't even the place he had planned!
> Can you believe the old rhyme says nothing of the sort,
> Or much of anything after Columbus left port?
> Here are the facts that will make you wonder
> Count the numbers, but don't go under!

The questions are embedded in the poem. Students' engagement was high during the class as they started to give their feedback to the poem. They read other materials and proceeded to write journal entries from the perspective of different people on the trip.

- How did Bartolome de Las Casas feel about the Taino people?
- How did Bartolome de Las Casas feel about Columbus and his men?

Once again, these sample open-ended questions allow students to create their own responses. Learning about perspectives also helps the students move to the type of thinking that helps them deepen their understanding.

In a middle school classroom, Mrs. Valone works with her students to learn about "tank man" (also known as "the unknown rebel"—the anonymous man who stood in front of a column of Chinese tanks the day after the infamous incident in Tiananmen Square). Her discussion about government includes academic questions such as:

- What is a government's purpose?
- What can citizens do when they are dissatisfied with the government?
- How can a government respond to the desires of the citizens?

Mrs. Valone projected the famous tank man image on the board. Students were engaged. Now questions moved to the following:

- What has happened?
- What is happening in this picture?
- Where was this picture taken?
- What does the red star symbolize?

She took an important step next and gave the students some priming, retrieval cues meant to help them figure out what they are seeing, so that their brains can try to interpret what they are taking in at the moment. Mrs. Valone used clues such as: it's a color photo and tank technology, to make connections for the students. This time, the engagement questions came after the students had been working through some of the foundational content. It is important to know that questions can call students to engage at any point in a lesson.

To engage learners in an alternative school in White Bear Lake, Minnesota, Mr. McGraw creates an economics unit that they won't forget. He opens with, "Has anyone here ever heard of the term 'microfinancing'?" From the varied answers he proceeds to the teaching portion of the lesson centered on the following questions:

- What is microfinancing?
- What is a microloan? (He starts with a great example to catch their interest of loaning a student $3.00 for lunch.)
- How are poor people already using financial services even though they are not members of a financial institution . . . a bank?
- Why won't banks serve poor people?
- If regular banking institutions are not designed to help the poor, how can some of them like the Grameen Bank of Bangladesh and Bancosol of Bolivia do it?
- What is "Kiva"?

From there, Mr. McGraw introduces how they are going to actually get involved as a class. They create a flea market to gain start-up money and then get involved with real-world, hands-on learning by making a microloan through Kiva to a "microentrepreneur" in need. This project originally started with Mr. McGraw's own question— "What if?"—for his class, and then grew to become so much more. The unit is full of questions and 21st-century skills, such as students asking, "How will I know to whom to loan my money?" Students in this alternative school—many of whom have not always liked school—can get involved in an experience that captures and engages their thinking. This unit starts by engaging students, but also helps students develop deep understanding that they may never have experienced if it wasn't for their work in Mr. McGraw's class.

Deepening Understanding

Remember back in Chapter 2 when Dylan Wiliam's (2011) ideas about discussion and diagnostic questions were presented? In social studies, there are often discussions that have to do with different perspectives. We can see students' thinking and learning when we interact with them around such questions. Wiliam used as an example (2011, p. 99):

> In which year did World War II begin?
>   a. 1937
>   b. 1938
>   c. 1939
>   d. 1940
>   e. 1941

He goes on to write about the differences we find in perspective about that question between Europe and America.

When we look into the classroom of Mr. Jacobs and his 10th-grade class in Ypsilanti, Michigan, they are focused on a unit about "the human commodity." Talk about our collective future! The students were being asked to think about hard concepts that have not been talked about commonly in their worlds. This is a low-performing, high-poverty school in the heart of the automotive economic collapse, and this young teacher has a great passion to have his students get excited about learning.

The "driving questions" were as follows:

- Who in the world today is being exploited?

- Where did modern slavery come from?

- What can we do?

In Mr. Jacobs's class, technology was used effectively to create a pre-assessment. The students answered individually online and then the pre-assessment became the centerpiece of the conversation the next day in class.

1. What is the average price of a slave today?
   a. $100
   b. $1,000
   c. $10,000
   d. $100,000

2. In the Trans-Atlantic Slave Trade, roughly 5 percent of slaves were shipped to America.
   a. True
   b. False

3. Which country founded the first forced labor plantation?
   a. America
   b. England
   c. France
   d. Portugal
   e. Spain

4. Slavery is still legal in some countries.
   a. True
   b. False

5. While mostly unsuccessful, slave mutinies aboard slaving ships saved an estimated 1 million Africans from slavery.
   a. True
   b. False

6. What was the most common way people in the Ancient World became slaves?
   a. Born to other slaves
   b. Captured after being born free
   c. Captured during war
   d. Convicted criminals

7. Where are the most slaves in the world today?
   a. Africa
   b. Asia
   c. Central America
   d. South America

8. Roughly how many slaves are there in the world today?
   a. 132,000
   b. 4.3 million
   c. 11 million
   d. 27 million

9. The United States of America currently has legislation against human trafficking.
   a. True
   b. False

10. The only full-scale slave rebellion that succeeded was
    in Haiti.
    a. True
    b. False

*FYI—the answers are 1, a; 2, a; 3, d; 4, b; 5, a; 6, b; 7, b; 8, d; 9, a;
and 10, a.*

Using these questions in a diagnostic way gave Mr. Jacobs critical formative information. Starting with the discussion and follow-up questions the next day, the class proceeded at a new level of engagement and learning. The students were so engaged that they concluded the unit with a "back-to-school" invitation to parents and the local newspaper to see the students' work. Unique for this school, the gathering allowed students to share and talk about their learning—and to demonstrate their deeper understanding.

One of the ways to deepen understanding is to use the Socratic method in a Socratic seminar. Socrates used questions to both invite the thoughts of those around him and for what it would do for a person's own thinking. The students sit in a circle and the teacher is outside the circle. Students come to the circle with the text read, and questions and insights prepared. Like most strategies in class, the students improve after they use the system a few times. This strategy can be adapted for any age group. Again, using YouTube as a resource, you can find helpful examples of the strategy being used by a myriad of age groups. Mr. Pears's 11th- and 12th-grade students in a comparative politics class use this structure often. Here is how questions can be seen as the core of the Socratic seminar.

Seminar selection: "Capitalism and Democracy" by
    Gabriel Almond

Topics: democracy, totalitarianism

Goal for skills: The students will start to develop their seminar skills of thinking interactively as well as citing the text to support claims.

Goal for content: The students will deepen their understanding of the dynamics of capitalism and democracy within a society.

Key concepts:
- democracy
- capitalism
- Marx
- socialism
- welfare state

Pre-activities: This lesson was actually going to be the first time the class used a Socratic seminar during this academic semester, so Mr. Pears wants student to be "set up for success" with their preparation.
- Students will complete an accompanying reading guide. Instructor will examine reading guides and provide feedback on the following areas:
  - Reading accuracy
  - Are there any glaring factual errors?
  - Did the student read the text and understand how the pieces fit together?
  - Does the student demonstrate how the argument builds upon itself?
  - Is there organization in their tracking document?

Seminar questions:
- Exploring questions
- What parts of the essay or specific vocabulary or sentences did you not understand?

- Students will share with the group
- Group will offer explanations about confusing concepts
- How does Almond organize his essay?
- How does Almond lay out his argument?
- Examining/core questions:
  - How does Almond say that capitalism supports democracy?
  - How does Almond say that capitalism subverts democracy?
  - How does he support his argument?
  - What is Friedman's argument on the greatest threat to democracy?
  - What is Mancur Olson's view on the relationship between a stable society and economic expansion? What evidence does he use to support his view?
  - What is Marx's view on the relationship of capitalism and democracy?
- Extending their thinking:
  - Does capitalism support or subvert democracy? Provide examples for your view.
- Students share their own questions

After every Socratic seminar, students spend time in a metacognitive exercise looking back on the experience and on their own thinking before and during the seminar.

Going Deeper: Metacognition

Encouraging students to take time to summarize, think about their own thinking and learning, and even plan their next steps is a valuable part of learning that sometimes gets missed because of a time crunch. When Shirley Clarke talks about strategies for enhancing learning in the primary grades, we believe she has uncovered a critical insight for all age levels of learners. "Encourage children to describe their efforts, ideas and products by asking open-ended questions—What can you tell me about...? How did you...? I notice you've ... what will you do next? This gives them the power to become self-evaluative" (Clarke, 2001, p. 127). This not only helps with the learning process itself, but also allows students to grow in their ability to articulate their thinking.

John Hattie has suggested that students may want to use these questions at the close of a lesson (2012, p. 48):

- What was today's goal?

- Did I achieve the goal? (From "not at all" to "fully")

- How much effort did I put in? (From "not much" to "a great deal")

For each of these questions, students would also incorporate their evidence from the day for their answer. This could be an exit slip or a journal entry. Either way, the teacher and student have documentation of their learning progress. Often, exit slips are used to track the content, but there is real power in knowing how the students perceive their thinking and learning in combination with what has been learned.

Anne Davies (2012) talks about a strategy that she calls "paired verbal fluency." Students work as partners. A timer is set for 45 seconds and student 1 speaks for that whole time on what he or she has learned during the lesson. Then student 2 has 45 seconds to talk, but it must be on different points than those made by student 1. The timer is set again for 30 seconds and each is again given a turn, with the direction that they must again use new talking points. The third and final round is for 15 seconds, with the same directions. Not only are the students helped with clarity about their thinking, but the teacher also gets a great formative picture of learning.

Figure 5.2 shows a template that has been used by psychology students after a project completed by partners. It gives a good summary snapshot of the process of the project. This template was originally adapted from Ted McCain's book *Teaching for Tomorrow* (2005). It has been very useful in helping students to think through those skills that they will need to use in collaborative work and in helping the teacher to see growth from project to project.

Mike Schmoker contends that there is a core of "versatile" questions that can be adapted for most any work. They are (2011, p. 153):

- Do you agree/disagree with the author?

- What inferences, interpretations, or connections can you make using the text?

- Do you approve or disapprove of this past or present policy, person, or movement? What lessons can we learn from it/them?

- What problem(s) does the study of this person or policy help or solve?

- What can we infer from this text about this particular time, place, or culture?

Whether you like these questions or those suggested as Essential Questions in the beginning of the chapter, the key is that we all should intentionally use questions in our classrooms.

The social studies classroom is a great place for questions. The examples in this chapter have shown a wide variety of uses of questions. It isn't important for you to always have such "different" questions for every lesson; the important thing is that the students know that you are a teacher who likes questions and who will listen as students give their insights when answering questions, and that students know their teacher will encourage each of them to ask their own questions.

FIGURE 5.2	Metacognitive Summary

Reflect on the process of doing the project. Write your responses for your work in the following areas:

Time Management (What have you learned that you would keep or change in your next project?)

Project Management (What did you learn about bringing all the different components of the project together?)

Research (What did you learn about the difference between gathering information and being able to use and apply relevant material?)

Project Design (What did you learn about the differences between the *process* of designing your project and what became your final *product*?)

Teamwork (What did you learn about teamwork during this project? Include what you learned about yourself as a team member.)

VIGNETTE
AN EXEMPLARY LESSON

Hayley Hook, a fourth-grade teacher at Columbus Elementary School in McMinnville, Oregon, had taken a class on powerful teaching strategies, hoping to improve her instructional methods. She also worked with an instructional coach, Amy Fast.

Hayley asked for Amy's coaching observations to be drop-ins. She wanted Amy to look for powerful questioning but did not want to know when Amy was coming because she wanted to gauge just how effective her questions were in her daily lessons.

Amy dropped in one time as Hayley was asking her students what some rules were that students must follow. Amy, the coach, assumed that students had probably gotten into trouble at lunch and that Hayley was going to review behavior expectations during social studies.

"Why do we have those rules?" Hayley asked. "Talk to your neighbor." And, then as always in Hayley's class, students turned to each other and began conversing easily and productively.

The students were sitting on the rug in the front of the room, and each and every student (all of whom were sitting cross-legged) instantly turned their bodies toward a partner so that their knees were nearly touching, set down whatever was in their hands, looked each other in the eyes, and began taking turns speaking and listening. After a few minutes,

"Okay" was all Hayley had to say, and all the students got quiet and shifted so that they were facing their teacher.

"What thoughts did you and your partner have?" she asked, calling on the students randomly.

The students mentioned the importance of being safe, the need for some sort of order, and the helpfulness of a common set of expectations. Then, Hayley placed a graph from the textbook on the document projector. It showed the amount of money that Oregon spends on the judicial, legislative, and executive branches of state government.

"On which branch of government in this state is most of our money spent according to the graph?" she asked. (The students had already studied the concept of the branches of government and were diving deeper into each this week.)

She waited a little while for students to study the graph, and then she asked, "Everybody?"

In choral response the students replied, "Legislative!"

"Now, why do you think that is? Turn to a partner." And the students were off again, shifting their bodies to analyze the question with their neighbors.

Hayley is one of those teachers who gets results. She believes that students need to learn to read out of textbooks and that learning in content areas cannot be comprised of only fun activities and simulations. She knows that in order for students to be post-secondary ready they must be able to pull out the meaningful information and synthesize the ideas presented in a text to make inferences about their learning. Thus, she relies heavily on powerful questioning to motivate and engage her students.

When this anticipatory set was over, the students went back to their assigned table groups and got their Cornell note templates out. (Throughout the day students are expected to take notes in each subject area. Their homework each night is to review their notes and write a summary about the learning that day that they felt was most important.)

Hayley asked them to review the previous day's learning with their table groups. What was most important? What were the main ideas? Specifically, what did they learn so far about the legislative branch? After calling on students randomly and checking for understanding, they were ready to begin new content.

Students took notes on the branches of the government while Hayley modeled taking notes. The first part of the textbook reading was about passing a local bill that would make the state nut the hazelnut.

"Why do you suppose both committees had to agree to pass the bill? Heads together..."

After groups had a chance to talk and share their ideas with the class, Hayley said, "Now I'm not sure that making the hazelnut the state nut is a very important bill. I'm sure it wasn't very hard for those committees to agree. Do you think there are some tougher decisions that our legislative branch has to make? What sorts of things would you imagine the two committees might not agree on? In what circumstances would it be hard for them to come to a decision?" Again students discussed their thoughts with each other before writing them down.

Hayley continued. "Let's bring it back to our own school. Let's say that you guys wanted to change something about our classroom and were going to present it to me in order to convince me that we should make the change. If everyone agreed on it and said it was a good idea—if the majority of the table groups thought it was a good idea—the change would be more likely to take effect. Let's connect this to our social studies learning. In your own words, why is having a majority in favor of a bill essential? Think about it for a bit and answer that question in your notes. Start with, 'Having a majority in favor of a bill is essential because...'" Hayley wrote the beginning of the sentence in her own notes, displayed, to help guide students.

As a class they continued to read out of the textbook, learning more about the branches of government. However, Hayley stopped often to ask powerful questions that related what they were learning to their own lives as citizens of Columbus Elementary.

At the end of the lesson Ms. Hook drew a Venn diagram on the board and asked students to do the same in their notes. Then she asked them to compare and contrast what they learned about the legislative and judicial branches of their government to their school's system for making and enforcing rules. One circle was "government" and the other was "school." Finally, she asked students to form an opinion on whether or not the school should be run more like the state government. As closure to the lesson, students had to state and defend their opinions with evidence from their textbooks.

Hayley then told the students that it was time for music class, and to put their notes and textbooks away. The students all groaned and said, "Do we have to?"

This may be a true test of powerful questioning—is it so engaging that students don't want to stop? And the teacher orchestrated the questioning while also using the textbook, often a maligned or misused resource.

VIGNETTE
RETHINKING OUR QUESTIONS
By an Instructional Coach

"But that isn't the way we have always done it," the middle school social studies teacher sighed for the third time since our meeting had started. "I know," I sympathized, "but what is it we really want them to know? Why do we even teach social studies in the first place?"

As an instructional coach for both elementary and middle school teachers, I had sat down to work with middle school social studies teachers to help create common formative assessments based on the social studies standards for our state and to assist them in designing new, interdisciplinary units that also weaved in the Common Core literacy and English language arts standards. To begin our work, we needed to dive into the standards and figure out what it really was that students needed to know. One of the first steps was to create Essential Questions that would not only guide all the teaching and learning within a unit—serving as the big picture—but would also be the cornerstone of the assessment.

The teachers were creating a unit test on the American Revolution, and we were at a standstill, staring at the Essential Question on the screen: *How have examples of cooperation and conflict during the era of the American Revolution impacted the course of American history?* One of the teachers muttered, "But this isn't how we do it.... Where are the questions that show us that they know the major political players of that time, the events leading up to the revolution, and when those took place? Isn't that what they need to know?"

Change is hard, so I thought carefully before continuing. "Well, what would they have to know and be able to do in order to answer that Essential Question? Wouldn't they have to know all of those things and understand the implications of them well? Wouldn't they have to analyze all of those facts and evaluate which ones had the most impact on the history of our country? Wouldn't they have to synthesize all of that new learning in order to answer that question? If they *were* able to answer that question and answer it well, would you know that they really 'got' one of the reasons we even study history in the first place?"

The teachers were still struggling, so I assured them that there definitely is a time and a place to ask fact-based questions. Of course there are things that students simply must *know*. After all, it is important for citizens of this country not to be ignorant of the facts. However, we cannot stop there. While it is important for us to know who signed the Constitution, isn't it even more important that we understand the ways in which we, as citizens, can affect the course of history, be inspired by revolutionary thinking and events of the past, and learn from mistakes that have been made? Isn't that why it is so important to study history anyway? Isn't that why our units, our day-to-day teaching and learning, and our assessments should all be framed by powerful questions? Just by asking the powerful question alone, we have answered powerful questions that students always have in their minds: Why should we learn this? Why should we care?

Powerful questions motivate students. They are powerful not just because they elicit critical thinking, but also because if the student can answer them, they themselves have gained a sense of power. If the saying "knowledge is power" is true, then imagine the influence of evaluation and synthesis. Students feel like they have one more piece of an important puzzle, one more insight into a complex world. They understand the implication of the learning, how it relates to their lives, and why they should care.

As I sat there with these teachers, who had a reputation for being amazing in the classroom, I couldn't help picturing where powerful questioning could take them and their students and just how phenomenal social studies could be. I envisioned all of the teaching and learning taking place under the umbrella of a few really powerful questions that were quite literally essential to the future success of these students and of our world. I pictured the result that combining these powerful questions with the Common Core literacy standards in social studies could have: students reading for meaning in order to prepare themselves for the heated debates, thought-provoking discussions, and purposeful writing that would ensue.

It is hard work rethinking the way we have always taught. It isn't that what we have been doing isn't good. It is that it could be *great*. And the difference between good and great could be as simple as the questions we ask.

CHAPTER 6

Powerful Questioning in Science

✑

"Science is facts; just as houses are made of stone, so is science made of facts; but a pile of stones is not a house, and a collection of facts is not necessarily science."

Jules Henri Poincaré
French mathematician

"In essence, science is a perpetual search for an intelligent and integrated comprehension of the world we live in."

Cornelis Bernardus Van Niel
U. S. microbiologist

Teacher and author Elizabeth Stein presents the following typical scenario in her article "Teaching Secrets: Asking the Right Questions" (2011).

> "The science lesson was in full swing when I walked into my inclusion class. The students seemed attentive, following along in their books as my coteacher read the science text aloud. Every so often, my coteacher paused to ask a question: 'What are renewable resources?' 'What are two examples of nonrenewable resources?' Students revisited

relevant sections of the text and eagerly raised their hands to answer. Afterward, the students were directed to reread the text, take notes, and respond to the questions at the end of the chapter.

"The students seemed to be on task—but how much were they learning?"

Stein's dilemma resembles countless other situations faced by teachers—the class is orderly and seemingly on task, students are participating, and the teacher is clearly in charge. However, Stein is right to question the cognitive impact of the instruction.

Later in Stein's article, she says, "So how can we break our patterns of asking recall-type questions? By weaving effective questioning techniques into our daily practice, we can create classroom environments that engage students in inquiry and problem-solving" (2011).

We, the authors, agree with Stein that effective questioning techniques are paramount in science instruction. With that being said, what exactly constitutes effective questioning in science?

Stein's article gives several highly practical tips: employ cooperative learning, encourage observation, teach students to ask their own questions, use formative assessment, and note what students are interested in, what they do, and what they say. She also advocates using several types of questions unlike the ones asked in the scenario that opens her article, including open-ended (or opinion-based) questions and elaboration questions.

Stein is right in advocating questions that are harder to answer than simple recall or "one right answer" questions, particularly in science. Science is, after all, a discipline built on the premise of inquiry. Let's examine the idea of scientific inquiry more deeply and consider the implications for science instruction.

The Role of Inquiry in Science Questioning

The *National Science Education Standards* define scientific inquiry as the diverse ways in which scientists study the world and propose explanations in addition to the activities of students in which they develop understanding of scientific ideas (National Committee on Science Education Standards and Assessment and National Research Council, 1996, p. 23). Inquiry is also described as a "multifaceted activity" that requires students to observe, question, explain, predict, and communicate (p. 23).

The National Science Teachers Association (NSTA) (2004) says that "understanding science content is significantly enhanced when ideas are anchored to inquiry experiences," recommends that "all K–16 teachers embrace scientific inquiry," and says that the NSTA "is committed to helping educators make it [scientific inquiry] the centerpiece of the science classroom."

Douglas Llewellyn, in his powerful book *Inquire Within*, calls questions "the language of inquiry" (2004, p. 127).

There is perhaps no other discipline that relies so heavily on questions, both those asked by teachers and those generated by students as they acquire and manipulate knowledge. With inquiry at the forefront, let us now turn to a discussion of questioning in the science classroom.

Teacher-Generated Questions

Remember the eight thinking moves cited in Chapter 1, from the excellent book *Making Thinking Visible* (Ritchhart, Church, and Morrison, 2011):

    1. Observing closely and describing what's there

    2. Building explanations and interpretations

3. Reasoning with evidence

4. Making connections

5. Considering different viewpoints and perspectives

6. Capturing the heart and forming conclusions

7. Wondering and asking questions

8. Uncovering complexity and going below the surface
   of things

These eight cognitive actions that teachers should desire in their students form a nice framework for designing questions in science. They are also well aligned with the discussions of inquiry and the "doing" of science in materials published by the National Science Teachers Association and other respected educational organizations.

Remember also the three purposes cited earlier in this book from Rothstein and Santana (2011): to engage students, to clarify thinking, and to deepen understanding. Science instruction can be wonderfully engaging when in the hands of effective teachers, and the questioning and dialogue that occur should lead students to become sharper in their reasoning and, as time goes on, to a deeper conceptual understanding of science content. However, in science, much like mathematics, periods of questioning directed by the teacher may be frustrating, because getting the "right" answer is not the primary objective—deep conceptual knowledge is the primary objective.

Laboratory work in science is a great opportunity for student-generated questions and true inquiry, but unfortunately it is an opportunity that is often squandered. In a position statement, the NSTA (2007) says that "developmentally appropriate laboratory investigations are essential for students of all ages and ability levels. They should not be a rote exercise in which students are merely following directions, as though they were reading a cookbook, nor should they be a superfluous afterthought that is only tangentially related to the instructional sequence of content."

Student-Generated Questions

Llewellyn (2004) distinguishes between information- and investigation-type questions that students create. This distinction is important for teachers to understand and to help their students understand, because true investigation questions are central to inquiry, and they are candidates for laboratory work.

Basically, investigation-worthy questions don't start with "why"; "why" questions are information-type questions (Llewellyn, 2004, p. 128). "Why" questions need explanations for answers. Investigation questions, on the other hand, often begin with "how," "what if," or "does," as in, "Does the surface area of an ice cube affect how fast it melts?" As Llewellyn notes, teachers may sometimes need to help students turn information questions into investigative ones, because they might not truly know what they are asking or what exactly is required or needed for an answer. He proposes three categories of questions, coming from either student or teacher or created collaboratively (2004, p. 129): those needing an expert to answer (information-type), those needing revision (investigation-type, but misstated as information-type), and those ready for investigation.

Typical Scenarios

Llewellyn provides an amusing yet far-too-familiar example of science-class discussion, excerpted below (2004, p. 130):

> The teacher, Mr. Poole, has distributed crackers to the students and has asked them to eat the crackers. As they start to chew, the discussion begins:

Teacher: What happens to the cracker as it enters your mouth? Can anyone tell me? (Calls on Student 1.)

S1: It's getting chewed.

T: It's getting chewed. Anything else?

S1: It's going to your stomach.

T: Before we get to the stomach, what's happening in your mouth? (Calls on Student 2.)

S2: There's that spit stuff working on it. (The class laughs.)

T: That's called saliva. Saliva moistens the cracker. Then what happens? Anyone? (Student 3 calls out.)

S3: It goes to your stomach?

T: No, before that.

S3: It goes down your esophagus?

T: Right. What happens after the esophagus?

While we applaud Mr. Poole for attempting to engage students in a demonstration, there is much to be desired in the questioning techniques employed even in this snippet of classroom discussion. This discussion is a classic example of "guess what's in the teacher's head," and is not illustrative of any aspect of inquiry or even of effective instruction in general. The questions Mr. Poole asks do not help the students clarify thinking or deepen understanding. One student doesn't know the simplest scientific terms well enough to use them without being prodded (saliva), and the student who does know some terminology (stomach, esophagus) is clearly unsure of the order of events in the process, as indicated by her rising voice, turning statements into questions. Mr. Poole is the person using most of the terminology, and he's not the one who needs mastery of these words. Also, the fully formed questions he does ask are vaguely worded ("What's happening in your mouth?") and represent only the recall level.

How could Mr. Poole's lesson have been improved, from the

standpoint of the teacher's questioning techniques? First, he could have done something at the beginning of the lesson to activate what the students already knew about the processes of digestion. He could have even had a simple advance organizer in the form of a word list posted on the board or screen: saliva, salivary glands, esophagus, stomach, peristalsis, gastric juice, mucus, duodenum, pancreas, small intestine, colon, etc. As students chewed, he could have had them work in pairs or triads with guiding questions such as, "What chemical changes to the cracker start happening as you chew?" and "Where does the substance go as you swallow?" Then he could have stopped periodically to check understanding by conducting short periods of whole-class discussion. As part of that discussion, students should be using the correct terminology and, perhaps, defining it in their own words and taking notes or drawing diagrams to become more actively involved in the learning. These are minor but rather easy-to-orchestrate changes that could improve engagement and clarity in this particular lesson. And, as Norton-Meier, Hand, Hockenberry, and Wise state, "If we as teachers have no control over what is going on inside an individual's head, then we have to be able to engage with learners in ways that make their knowledge the center of the conversation" (2008, p. 15). In Mr. Poole's class, the knowledge of the students was not the center of the conversation—as a matter of fact, it was difficult to even discern what students knew versus what they were guessing.

Let's examine another very typical lesson, but again, one in which the questioning could be revised for greater effectiveness. This particular lesson takes place in a 7th-grade classroom.

Class begins, and the teacher asks students to "settle down" and get out their notebooks so they can refer to notes taken on the previous day.

Teacher: We've been studying animal cells. Let's review. Let's start with what we already knew about plants before we got to animals. Who remembers the function of the stomata?

Student 1: It does something with the gases in photosynthesis.

T: Yes, that's right, it's called gaseous exchange. What about plant cells? Who remembers how they are different from animal cells?

Student 2: They have cell walls. Animal cells don't.

Student 3: They have chloroplasts, right?

T: You're both right. What are chloroplasts?

Student 4: They have chlorophyll.

T: Yes, they do, but is that what they are? I'm looking for what they are.

S3: They do the photosynthesis. That's where it happens.

The next few minutes of the lesson proceeded in a similar fashion, with the students making unsubstantiated or vague statements, and the teacher asking questions that required very little in terms of knowledge or reflection.

Just down the hall, however, another 7th-grade science teacher was starting her review in a different way. She began by asking this of the entire class: "Think of just one part of a plant cell ... mitochondria, cell membrane, nucleus, cell wall, vacuole, and so on.... Now think about the human body, its organs, systems, functions, and parts. After you think a bit, fill in the following frame: 'The (plant cell/part) is like the (human body organ/system/function/part) because....' Create at least one sentence. You may work with a partner."

Students huddled with partners, opened their textbooks, talked, flipped through their notebooks, and all hurriedly tried to create an analogy.

In about three minutes, the teacher began calling on students, saying, "Can you give us your analogy?"

The first student called upon didn't have a complete analogy but said that he and his partner were trying to compare photosynthesis to the actions of the lungs in the human body.

"Okay, let's keep hearing from others," the teacher responded. "Perhaps you'll be able to flesh out that analogy."

The next student compared the stomata to skin and used the word "epidermis." The teacher asked, "What is the function of the stomata?"

The student answered, "It exchanges the gases in photosynthesis and it's on the outside of the leaf."

The teacher then asked, "Is it like something in or on our skin?" Excitedly, the student's partner said, "Is it a pore? Pores are holes in our skin, and stomata are like holes on a leaf."

"Let's pursue that, the pore idea," said the teacher. "Does a pore exchange gases?"

The student turned to her partner, who said, "I don't think so."

The teacher then told that pair to go into their textbook to find the answers. She also told the rest of the class, "I'll give you two more minutes to make your analogies."

Upon convening whole-class discussion again, the boy from the pair of students that had been working on the stomata/pore analogy said, "I still believe stomata are like skin, more like the pores. They both release bad things from the leaf and from the body."

The teacher asked, "Could you explain?"

The teacher guided the next part of the discussion, focusing on why each of the structures is important, helping the pair of students to sharpen their analogy. The final analogy was, "Stomata in a plant are like pores in our skin because both maintain a heat balance in the organism."

Which class would you rather be a student in? Obviously, the review in the second classroom was far more engaging, and the cognitive work deeper.

Improving Questioning in Science Instruction

Principal Majalise Tolan, from Lincoln County, Oregon, has supported teachers in improving their questioning across the curriculum. She generated this list of what effective teachers do with science inquiry (2012):

- They are not afraid of silence. They often present information and then allow students to be confused (in a good way). They don't feel the need to give the "answers" and instead let the students struggle cognitively. Related to this, they create learning environments in which it's safe to not know the "right" answer.

- They are confident in their own abilities as inquirers and in their skills as teachers.

- They plan ahead for the questions students might have to help better facilitate their learning.

- Laboratory experiences are not predetermined to a high level of specificity. Materials are ready, and the teachers help students carry out the labs, but there is a true sense of investigation.

- Students answer authentically and don't just mimic the teacher's language. An observer can tell that kids "own" the learning.

We can extrapolate from this list the following reminders about effective questioning in science:

- Periods of silence are okay during any segment or type of science lesson. The old guidelines (Rowe, 1986) about providing at least three full seconds of wait time do apply—at a minimum. If you're asking hard questions, or if students are engaged in observations, labs, etc., then ideal "think" time may be even longer.

- Not knowing for certain why something might be or what might happen "if . . ." is a mental disposition that is very important in science learning.

- The teacher must be a model of inquiry at all times.

- Preplanned questions are necessary for classroom discourse. It's very difficult to emphasize the habits of mind and to deepen conceptual understanding if questions are developed "on the fly." Likewise, assessment items and tasks must focus on questions that are application-level or higher on Bloom's Taxonomy.

- Laboratory work should mirror the work of real scientists as much as possible. This means students are seeking to answer investigation questions, not information questions.

- Students must use the language of the discipline in speaking and writing and must engage in authentic reading tasks that require knowledge of science terminology. Deep understanding of science demands that students understand the most important terminology at the expressive level—meaning they not only know what the words mean when they see them in text, but that they can *use* those words correctly themselves.

If a teacher is to act on these reminders, then he or she must be supported first by others who can help discover the questioning patterns and techniques already in place. As many educators know, it's incredibly difficult to monitor one's questioning when one is busy teaching and responding to what seems like a thousand stimuli per minute. Colleagues or supervisors can be of great help; with their outside perspectives, they can observe things about your questioning habits that are hard to monitor yourself. Recall the instructional coach mentioned earlier in the book who pointed out to a teacher, much to his surprise, that he had not asked a single question during a 30-minute lesson.

Scenarios

Examine this exemplary middle school science lesson for the power of the questioning within it. Here is the context. There are 20 students in grade 7, ages 12 and 13, who make up this integrated science class. This particular class generally works very well with classroom discussion because many of them are auditory learners. Seven students have individualized education programs that require modifications with reading and scribing. The teacher requires verbal discussion in full sentences. An observer will hear the word "because" and other transitional words that enable students to submit their contributions in full sentences. The student population is from a high-poverty area, and thus much attention is also given to academic vocabulary.

The primary content goal for this instructional sequence is to determine what students already know about energy transfer and kinetic molecular theory. A secondary content goal is to help students work like scientists, using an intentional scientific method and specific process skills. Students must collaborate and have a sense that scientists are members of a scientific community as opposed to picturing a guy with crazy hair working alone to build a monster in his basement. A tertiary goal is to embed literacy strategies not only in written responses but also in spoken responses. Figure 6.1 shows the lesson design sequence.

The teacher noted that kinetic molecular theory is an abstract concept; it takes multiple experiences for students to process and explain it with accuracy. She also noted that a fruitful academic discussion requires more than talking; it requires listening and analyzing the contributions of others. The teacher's expectations in this regard are very well aligned with the collaboration and speaking standards in the Common Core.

The students entered the class and took about five minutes to complete a bell-ringer exercise. Bell ringers are to be completed in full sentences using correct sentence structure.

The initial understandings and misconceptions the students expressed after the bell ringer activity were as follows:

Cody stated that "heat goes to the bottom and cold goes to the top." He was attempting to make a connection to what he remembered about convection currents in the mantle of the earth. It is likely that he was remembering that magma rises because of the increased temperature and when it reaches the top of the mantle the temperature decreases and it falls again. This concept of the effect of heat on molecular motion also applies to other areas of science. It is important to look for opportunities to repeat abstract concepts like this one in multiple contexts.

Moe revealed a common misconception as well, when he stated that "air is trying to escape" the teakettle. Students think that *all* bubbles are "air"; it is not unusual that even though several of them used the term "evaporation," they have not yet made the connection that the "vapor" in evaporation is water vapor, thus the bubbles in the teakettle are still water molecules. The teacher made a note of this very

FIGURE 6.1   **Lesson Design Sequence**

1. Sponge Activity	2. Real-World Application	3. Real-World Application (continud)
Bell Ringer 9-13-11 LEVEL 0 USING Science-specific words, EXPLAIN what is causing the bubbles to form. _____ _____ _____ _____ _____	Consider this … 	Consider this …

4. Exit Slip Side 1	5. Exit Slip Side 2	6. Demonstrate Heat Transfer
Name_____ Class_____ Date_____ Which teakettle has more kinetic energy? I know this because … [box]	Imagine that you work at a party store during the summer. You and the owner are going to deliver some party balloons to a birthday party. The delivery car has been sitting in the hot sun all day long. The owner tells you to inflate a big bunch of balloons but advises you not to inflate the balloons all the way. **Provide a detailed scientific explanation of why the owner's advice is wise.** _____ _____ _____ _____ _____	20° room temperature 5°C 35°C

7. Experiment Heat Transfer	8. Data Equilibrium Graph	
	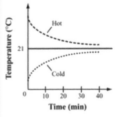	

common misconception for when the class moved to its unit on properties of matter. For now, the focus is energy.

David made this contribution: "The fast-moving molecules are trying to move out and the slow-moving molecules are trying to move in." This particular misconception is quite common and was later addressed with a demonstration in which students observed and recorded temperatures of hot and cold water in separate containers (see frame 6). They observed that heat moves in predictable ways, always transferring from hot objects to cold objects. Students have a difficult time with this concept, because they are accustomed to feeling cold objects and think that the cold is moving into their hands. They have heard terms such as "cooling off" or "letting cold air in." These phrases often cause a misconception that heat moves out and cold moves in, as David stated. The lab setup (in frame 7) was designed to demonstrate that heat energy always moves from hot objects to cold objects until equilibrium is reached.

Students continued to form testable hypotheses about how to "make a better bubble." After testing all of the bottles available, they concluded that the plastic water bottle made the better bubble because the bubble, although small, formed faster and lasted longer.

The digital photo of the hot air balloon (frames 2 and 3) was used to link back to the content probe using a real-world application. This required students to go back into their working memory and apply the concepts of heat energy and molecular motion to a real-world application. It was during this portion of the discussion that students began to reveal more misconceptions they had about thermal energy. There were some students that thought the heat energy applied to the gas in the balloon caused the molecules to expand. This misconception surfaces when the container used is flexible, unlike the glass bottles used in the demonstration.

The teacher was thrilled that students had applied their prior knowledge of convection currents with this degree of success. When the teacher felt the students were heading off track, she simply repeated her initial statement, "Explain what is happening inside the teakettle."

The teacher repeats and sometimes paraphrases student responses. This is intentional and is done to make sure all in the room heard the response and, equally importantly, to give students processing time before the teacher continues probing a given question or changes the question.

Once the teacher uncovered the misconceptions that she was expecting about the teakettle, she moved to the bottle, because the matter involved now does not involve a phase change, so this offers a different scenario to probe. The teacher wanted to present heat energy transfer in several settings to uncover as many misconceptions and as much prior knowledge as possible.

The new probe was, "What is happening inside the bottle?" There was a significant amount of discussion about evaporation until Brandon stated, "The heat from the water is causing the air inside the bottle to want to come out." He got the ball rolling and the teacher thought the class was headed toward molecular motion and kinetic energy and prompted him to tell me why. Jasmine intervened and sent him back to evaporation. So, the probing continued, as the class had to circle back to evaporation. The teacher asked Brandon, "So what *is* evaporation?" This was an attempt to show that there was no water in the bottle to undergo evaporation.

Shelbie weighed in and brought this to light. She stated that the hot water turned from liquid to a gas. The teacher replied, "Is there any hot water in the bottle?" Now, they are back again to the original question, "What is happening inside the bottle?" Jasmine said earlier, "The bubble is *evidence* of what is happening inside the bottle." Then Cody said, "The heat is making the molecules move faster and want to go outside the bottle and the only way out is the opening, so they are pushing the bubble."

Some of the students in the video segment alluded to physical properties and phase changes when referring to cold as "heavier" than hot. The teacher intervened to bring the topic back to kinetic energy by repeating what David had said earlier, "Heat causes molecules to move fast and cold causes molecules to move slow." In the end, students come to the understanding that on the molecular level, heat and motion are the same. This is repeated several times and will culminate at the end of the unit.

Most students seem to have a basic intuitive understanding that heat is related to fast molecular motion and cold is related to slow molecular motion. They do, however, have misconceptions about the composition of the bubbles in boiling water, the distinction that heat is energy and although it has an impact on matter, it is not matter in itself, and the understanding that hot objects always transfer energy to cold objects.

Finally, the exit slip (frames 4 and 5) was assigned to bring the lesson back to independent practice. The exit slip mimics the format of an extended response, like those used in the state assessment. The teacher used it as a vehicle for writing to demonstrate learning and to uncover additional misconceptions.

The students had significant success with this investigation, which included graphing their results to visualize a typical equilibrium graph (frame 9). This lab was followed up with an extended response to explain the data and results.

For all classes that the teacher taught the lesson to, the results were as follows:

20 distinguished, 72 proficient, 38 almost proficient, 14 not proficient. Students need and will get repeated exposure to the concept of heat transfer from hot to cold or from "fast molecules to slow molecules."

Scenario: Powerful Questioning in Action

The middle school science teacher stood outside the door, and students gathered around. (This was routine/protocol from day one … it doesn't occur every day, and not always with every class, but it occurs regularly.) The teacher asked each student a question as he or she entered the room; sometimes it was simply a recall/review question; other questions led to great discussions once all were in the classroom. Even the lower-level/recall questions, though, were used as a quick way to address misconceptions and, in some cases, led to a new learning that, although it wasn't a part of that day's lesson, was something that they took the time to explore because it deepened students' understandings of the things they were studying.

The teacher asked, "What is the job of a chloroplast?" The student happened to answer partially incorrectly, and stated that it was where chlorophyll was made. The teacher was looking for, "It's the place in the cell where photosynthesis takes place." Instead of letting this go, she brought it back into the classroom and asked students why they thought a wrong answer was given. The student was never named and no attention was drawn to him. In discussion, students addressed the idea of the prefix "chloro-," which means green.

Another student mentioned that it can be confusing because chlorophyll is needed for photosynthesis and it is found in the chloroplasts. Another student blurted out, "Oh! I was a bit confused about chloroplasts, chlorophyll, and photosynthesis." The teacher asked if a few others were wondering about the same things; several hands went up. She then took the time to work through the creation of a labeled diagram with accompanying word map about how chlorophyll, found in the chloroplasts, is responsible for absorbing the light (with the exception of the green spectrum) that is used in photosynthesis. She did not draw out the diagram; it was a class effort that she guided by asking questions ... "What might we do to make this more understandable?" "How would a word map help?" "Would you like to begin a word map for us?" "Some of you feel a diagram of a chloroplast would also be helpful ... what structures should we include? Any volunteers to draw while we contribute?"

None of the questions were particularly high level at this point, but when they were finished, one student asked about fall.

The teacher said, "What do you mean?"

"What happens in the chloroplast when it is fall? The leaves don't stay green."

Another student pointed out that they learned in elementary school that the trees don't produce chlorophyll in the fall, that's why the leaves turn color.

"Okay, so does that mean the trees die each fall?" replied the first student, somewhat sarcastically.

The teacher stepped in here, turning this into a productive discussion that deepened students' knowledge about photosynthesis.

"Do they die? What do we know about photosynthesis?" She directed it back to the word map; students came to realize the connection between waning daylight hours, less chlorophyll produced, and less light absorbed, and so leaves begin reflecting more than just the unabsorbed green light.

As stated earlier, there is perhaps no other discipline that relies so heavily on questions as does science. Inquiry is the heart of science, and powerful questioning by teachers is critical so that students learn to be inquirers, observers, and questioners themselves. We end this chapter with an observation of a teacher as she engages in the "real science" of questioning in her elementary classroom.

FIGURE 6.2 **Observation Data**

Observation of Teacher Hayley Hook
by Amy Fast, Instructional Coach

MATH REVIEW

"Why don't we use square centimeters?"

"Who can turn this information into something that will help us solve the problem?"

"Heads together: What is the name of the next model?" ("I'm going to pull a stick this time.")

"Why is it called a 'model'?" . . . "I heard you say the word 'shows'—good."

"What is the equation that matches this model? Everybody answer." (choral response)

"I hear some disagreement. Why do you think your answer is right?"

"How can you convince me your answer is right?"

"What is the property this model is showing?"

"If we are using the number line to show a multiplication equation, where does the number line need to start?"

"Why would it be a problem to start a number line at the number 2? Heads together."

"What is the area of the next model?"

SCIENCE

"As he is showing us this, I want you to be thinking about: How does it work?"

"Ethan brought this in for a purpose. What do you think is happening here, energy-wise?"

"Both kinds of energy fall under what general title?"

FIGURE 6.2 **Observation Data** *(continued)*

INTRODUCED OBJECTIVE: *"What's the Matter?"*

"What is matter?"

"How do you know that?"

SLIDE SHOW ON MATTER

Matter is anything that takes up space.

"Take one of these images and defend why it would be considered matter."

Matter is made up of all things, living and nonliving.

"What are living and nonliving things?" (One student says, "Hey, I take up space and I'm living ... I must matter," leading to smiles all around.)

"Can you come up with your own examples of matter?"

"How are those both examples?"

"What are the differences between how the particles move in a solid, liquid, or gas?" (to be learned)

"What is a hypothesis?"

We are going to form our hypotheses on this question. Go back to your desks and get your homework journals out. I see three people that are ready ... table two is ready ... Max, will you please move table one and table two forward?

The class produces Cornell notes on what has been learned so far (modeled by teacher while students take notes in their own journals).

FIGURE 6.2 **Observation Data** *(continued)*

Coach's Summary of Data

Research on this power strategy states that "no more than 50 percent of the questions you ask should be strictly factual."

- 12 out of the 22 questions asked during the observation (55 percent) were considered "powerful questions."

The research also suggests the use of mandates to engage students when asking the questions.

- The teacher used collaborative learning, such as "think-pair-share" and note-taking.

In addition, the research on powerful questioning states that teachers should provide at least three seconds of wait time after asking a question.

- Students had at least three seconds to process each question asked by the teacher.

Finally, the research suggests finding a way to call on all students by using popsicle sticks with students' names on them pulled randomly out of a jar for each question and then set aside.

- The teacher did this consistently in her lesson.

The teacher demonstrated all of the critical attributes of powerful questioning.

VIGNETTE

HOW I CAME TO ASK BETTER QUESTIONS

By Lisa Cebelak

I remember that day well. I was exhausted and I had lost my voice, again. I sat at my teacher desk after school reflecting on the day. Once again, I felt like I had worked really, really hard. And my students, well, I am pretty sure they just sat there. I mean, I was on my feet all day! Every class, I was in front of the classroom, working and lecturing, greeting students and following up with absent students, making sure they knew what they missed. I was busy, busy, busy. I was active. And that was the big problem. *I* was the one being active. My students, on the other hand, were being passive. I thought about it while drinking a bottle of water. My throat was sore.

About that same time, my principal had asked the high school staff—I was a high school English language arts teacher at the time—to fill out a personal teaching goal for the year. It had been due yesterday. It sat on my desk and I knew I had to fill it out, but wanted to make sure it was a teaching goal I would really want to work on. It also had to be measured in some way. That is when it came to me. I knew I wanted to have a goal that had me working smarter, and my students working more. But, how do I word that on paper, on a teacher goal form? How does one measure that?

When my colleague, a fellow English teacher, came into my room, I tried to tell her about my teaching goal. In my scratchy voice, I tried to articulate my idea. She responded, "You need to talk less, and have your students talk more." I realized her comment was dead on. I was talking too much, lecturing too much, providing too much information. My students had learned to wait me out. If they sat there, passively, I would do the work.

I thought about how much time I spent talking during a typical class period. Have you ever thought about that? What percentage of the time during a class period do you spend talking? I guessed that I talked about 80 percent of the time. I talked too much! Whoa—time to change.

I wrote my personal teaching goal for the year. It was simple. I would share the speaking responsibility with my students. I would talk 50 percent of the time in class and have my students take on the other 50 percent. My students needed to speak up and collaborate more. It was a great goal. It was a measurable goal (through observation). It was a goal that was more challenging to meet than I ever thought it would be. It was also a goal that changed my teaching forever.

The first few weeks were a total disaster. I remember at one point asking my students a question and they all just sat there, waiting. Waiting me out. It was the most awkward silence I had ever experienced. They were supposed to talk and explain and, well, elaborate on my question, and yet—nothing. I think fifteen seconds went by. I knew the average wait time was three seconds, so this was an eternity. The problem was twofold: I had asked a very specific question that there was only one right answer to. And, my students were used to me giving the answer when no one spoke up. I had two things I had to fix. I had to ask better questions, open-ended questions. And, I had to change the culture of my classroom. Well, I certainly was learning a lot in those first few weeks.

After failing, and failing again, I learned what didn't work. And from there, I changed my teaching practices until something did start to work. The first time I asked an open-ended question, while teaching *The Great Gatsby*, by F. Scott Fitzgerald, I started to get a few responses. The question was "How hard is it to move from one social class to another?" I asked students to talk with an elbow partner for a few minutes and write down at least one idea. I called on certain students to share out loud and started to get some pretty interesting responses. One student talked about the "99 percent" and the "Occupy" protests that were starting to occur at the time. This led to a lot of nodding and questions about what is going on in the news. Another student discussed how his dad lost his job and about how he considered his family to be of middle class stature last year, but now his dad was unemployed and they were about to lose their house. This led to a discussion about the economy and how some people go "down" a class instead of up. Another student raised the point that too many people are trying to keep up with the Joneses, and that people just aren't satisfied with what they have. As each student spoke up, I saw the engagement of other students as they "tuned in" to what was being said. I realized the power of peers in that moment. I noticed that teenagers had a lot of questions themselves and wanted to talk about them, but needed a venue for the conversations to occur.

Before this discussion occurred, I am sure many of my students were not excited to read *The Great Gatsby*. But now

I had students discussing social class, and in such depth that they could go back and give me examples from the text and were actually eager to share connections to what was going on locally or globally in the news. And all of this stemmed from asking *one* question. I remember I didn't get to my teaching objectives that day; I got carried away in the discussion of the aspects of social class. Not only were my students engaged, but I was engaged as well. I was excited to teach and was watching my students discuss and critically think as I simply nudged them here and there. The more I stayed out of the conversation, the more they talked. When the bell rang, I had a few students comment how fast class went that day. As a high school teacher, I can promise you that those are beautiful words to hear.

From that day on, I was bit by the bug to ask better questions. It was like I unlocked a secret to great teaching. I learned to base my lesson plans and units on creating quality questions to pose in the classroom. I knew that sometimes it would only take one question. One question could transform the culture of my classroom. One question could lead to critical thinking. One question could engage students like never before. One question that I asked that would allow me to listen, instead of talk. Powerful questioning can do all that.

CHAPTER 7

Powerful Questioning in Other Content Areas

꙳ঌঌ৹ঌ꙳

"More effort needs to be given to framing questions that are worth asking."

John Hattie
(2012, p. 75)

Effective questions are the core of dialogue between teachers and students. This dialogue leads to interdisciplinary work, application of skills, acquisition of life skills, and connection with students.

Marzano and Heflebower (2012) point to work done by Marzano and Kendall in 2007 to update the taxonomy of skills and knowledge base necessary for today's students. They include four types of knowledge: 1) factual, 2) conceptual, 3) procedural, and 4) metacognitive (Marzano and Heflebower, 2012, p. 10). These fall into two categories, referred to earlier in this book: cognitive and conative. It is the conative category that seems especially important to the work done in elective classes. "Conative skills refer to one's ability to analyze situations in light of what one knows and how one feels and select appropriate actions" (p. 10). The elective courses in every school open for students a great opportunity for immediate engagement, since they choose which courses to take according to their interests. Electives also bring together the four types of knowledge in practical ways.

The lessons and strategies in this chapter represent the intersection of many skills and types of thinking, including all the types of knowledge, and both conative and cognitive skills.

The most effective teachers seize any opportunity to move beyond mere "information gathering" to focus on building on students' foundation of knowledge. We must teach students to *apply* the information that has been gathered. As you read through examples from teachers in various disciplines, note how questions are used in a myriad of ways to engage students in the learning process.

In Ms. Nelson's art class for grades 9–12 students, the lesson focuses on the work of Piet Mondrian.

The class opens with the teacher simply asking the class directly, "What is the 'question' of Mondrian's work?" Students first do a "think-pair-share" to respond. In several minutes, the teacher brings them back to interact as a whole class. The consensus is reached that the artist's goal is to reduce everything to its simplest form. Students are shown several examples in a PowerPoint presentation of his work. For each example, the students are asked, "What do you see?" and the engagement is high. The students are set free to work on the painting assignment of the day with, "How would you paint one floor of your house in a Mondrian style?" Students get busy talking with each other—about what they were seeing, about color, and about how they would move from sketch to painting in the block style. High engagement has been achieved by setting the stage with questions that lead to more questions, this time from the students themselves.

Questions lead to wonder, wonder leads to questions, and both lead to learning.

In Ms. Strand's personal finance business class for grades 9–12, questions help students open their perspectives on real-life problem-solving challenges.

When teaching about the teen version of *Who Moved My Cheese?* by Spencer Johnson, her reflective questions are a key. Notice as you read these questions that the prompts connect the students to life experience and previous knowledge. Note prompt number six in particular; it helps students make a prediction, which draws them to think in deeper, more critical ways. Here are some of the questions she uses:

1. At the beginning of the book, Hem and Haw become so comfortable, they don't notice what is happening. Realizing that they don't know where the cheese comes from, who puts it there, or that it's slowly getting smaller, they respond to the circumstances. Are there times in your life when you act like Hem and Haw in this situation, perhaps taking something for granted or assuming something will always be there?

2. "It's not fair!" In what situations do you think or say this? Now looking back, what do you learn about the effectiveness of this method for dealing with change?

3. The fear we let build up in our minds is often worse than the situation that actually exists. As you look back, when have you felt this way and what can you learn from it?

4. Has someone tried talking you out of making a positive change in your life simply because you or they were afraid? What was the situation? What did you learn about decision making/risk taking that still stands out to you?

5. Fear can keep us from moving forward and achieving our goals. When do you see fear play this role for you or someone important to you? What are you learning?

6. When looking for New Cheese, Haw kept thinking about what he could gain instead of what he was

losing. Why do you suppose we often think that
change will lead to something worse?

7. Fear can be good if it prompts us to action. When
does fear prompt you to take action/control—to do
something, rather than simply letting things happen?

Ms. Strand's questions guide students to interact with the text, incorporating their own experience and the experiences of others. Ms. Strand is excited to share some of the rich conversations she had with students as a result of these prompts.

When we encourage students to write about their experiences, to "think through the end of a pen" (a favorite quote of Dr. Douglas Reeves attributed to author Stephen King) or to summarize their thinking, we are doing critical work to help students think and learn; this in turn helps these same students' achievement scores rise.

As Mr. Sill's International Baccalaureate business class students collect their thinking during one particular lesson, they see market analysis at work. Mr. Sill is about to have the class read the article "Lego is for Girls" by Brad Wieners, which appeared in *Bloomberg Businessweek* in 2011. Focusing on boys saved the toymaker in 2005, but now the company needs to crack the code for "the other 50 percent of the world's children." This whole lesson captures the students' interest, as this is something from their own childhood. Note the following questions that were used as the anticipatory set to engage the learner.

• From ages 5 to 12 what were the top five toys you
played with?

• By a show of hands, how many of you owned Legos at
some point in your life? (Even as you read this, can

you think of anyone who wasn't fascinated with Legos?)

- Who is the target market for Legos?

- How did you come to this conclusion?

- What has Lego done to reinforce your assumption?

- If you were to choose a new demographic for Lego to target, who would you suggest? Why?

- If you were to develop a marketing plan to reach that market, approximately how much would you budget to spend?

- What about targeting girls? What modifications, if any, would you make to make the product appealing to girls?

- Imagine watching a group of girls ages 5 to 12 and a group boys ages 5 to 12 construct a Legos box … what observations do you think you would make?

What do you notice about these questions? Here are some key features:

1. The questions are used as an invitation to learning. The questions first have students sharing their experiences, but then have them recognizing how many factors go into marketing decisions.

2. The questions connect the students to their experiences and to each other. There is common experience, and the learning community is strengthened as the students learn.

3. The questions engage the students in asking their own questions. From this lesson, the students develop

the questions that they still need to answer if they were to get ready to build a marketing plan of their own.

The questions in the examples we've just read are used in very intentional ways. These questions are integral to student thinking and learning. These questions engage learners in an art class, clarify thinking in Ms. Strand's personal finance class, and deepen understanding in Mr. Sill's business class. Next we'll focus on experiential learning in a consumer living classroom.

Electronic Portfolio in Consumer Living

Ms. Market has her consumer living students go to elementary schools to apply what they have learned about child development in the classroom (the portfolio guidelines and rubric are available in Appendix B).

Reflective questions are critical as the students think through the experiences they are having. Teaching students about reflections is a core part of this experience. Ms. Market has students spend extended time in an elementary classroom. She instructs each student to build an electronic portfolio as the documentation of their work. Reflective questions are a component of each area of their portfolios. They first define reflection, then answer the first critical question, "Why is reflection so important?" With that, she sets the frame for their work. The students reflect using these questions:

- What went well?

- What didn't work the way you hoped?

- What would you change for another time?

- How would this work influence how you parent or perhaps lead a classroom someday?

- What did you learn?

Students realize that they need to pause and reflect, not just finish the day in the class and speed to the next experience. Questions create the frame through which to take that pause.

Electronic Format for Responses to a Video Clip

Mr. Lee uses technology effectively as a learning tool with his middle school students: he frames what the students will be looking for and has them use their iPads to actively respond to what they are seeing and hearing. Technology used in this way goes beyond "searching for information"—it effectively becomes part of the thinking and learning process. Mr. Lee describes it this way:

> I start a discussion thread and explain to the kids what they are expected to do, which can vary from video to video. I basically am asking them to ask and respond to questions during the video. I will usually stop the video a short way in to make sure everyone has posted a question or comment. Schoology allows the instructor to see who has and hasn't posted. Once they get the ball rolling, it is pretty amazing how wrapped up they get in both the video content and their discussions. Once the video is over, I have them take a moment to scan through comments and make a last post. I, as the instructor, join them and identify a few posts that seem to be popular within the discussion (have the most responses). We then discuss these few questions out loud and see where they take us. Ultimately, I tie it in to the essential learning for the day.

This is an activity that requires each student have access to the discussion board. It is very straightforward for most students. As students watch the video as a class, they should make comments or ask questions as they come to mind. The teacher can choose to pause the video as needed to allow time for students to complete their thoughts. Every time students post, the thread refreshes. They can see if someone has responded to their post and thus reply again. This all happens very quickly, so the instructor must hit F5 or click refresh frequently to monitor the discussion.

Mr. Lee shares what this looks like using Schoology in Appendix C. In this video discussion, we clearly see him create a frame for student viewing that has as its goal that students would post insights and ask questions. This allows them to clarify their own thinking, deepen their understanding about the information as they ask their own questions, and stay engaged, in part because of the immediacy of responses from the other students and the teacher. Engagement is high as the students focus on thinking and learning.

In each window we look through into these classrooms we see active learning. We see questions coming from teachers as they frame the learning, and then from students as they *own* the learning.

CRITICAL QUESTIONS AT C.L.A.S.S.

By Camilla Sutherland and Pat Flattley

The Central Learning Adult/Alternative School Site (C.L.A.S.S.) in Fresno, California is unique in that there are two schools on one site. The Central Learning Alternative School Site is a hybrid independent study program serving mainly high school students. Students are scheduled to meet with their core teacher a minimum of once weekly, and if enrolled in mathematics they attend whole-class instruction on a separate day. The Central Learning Adult School Site is located on the same campus. The adult learning program started in the 1970s and has been an exemplary program for years. Several academic programs are offered, including completion of high school diploma; General Equivalency Diploma preparation; and remediation of basic academic skills. There are also program-specific avenues for certified nursing assistant, auto body repair welding, and office professional, in addition to other general courses for adult learners.

Improving student achievement is an ongoing discussion among faculty members. During the weekly professional learning community (PLC) meetings, questions came up regarding students not being able to pass the unit or chapter tests, thus preventing them from earning credits. Teachers shared that it was frustrating seeing students being able to complete the homework and not pass the tests. Different practices were discussed, but consensus on a best practice was never finalized.

At about this same time, faculty members and the director attended an in-service program about English Language Learners. Writing strategies were mentioned often in this program. The information was then shared and discussed at the next few PLC meetings. Teachers agreed that the C.L.A.S.S. student population has gaps in English skills and that using ELL instructional strategies would be best for all students.

The director researched three years of California High School Exit Examination data specific to English language arts and found that students scored significantly lower in the writing standards and writing conventions strands than in the other three strands. Teachers then engaged in several professional development sessions on writing.

Then teachers developed a set of critical questions—questions that cannot be answered simply with a "yes" or "no." These critical questions became part of our school culture.

1. Cite one fact/thing you learned from your reading this week.

2. Determine the central idea(s) of the text.

3. Draw evidence/example(s) from the text to support the central idea.

4. Identify the author's purpose and/or point of view. Explain the text/literary devices used.

5. Evaluate the reasoning (pros and cons) and evidence (proof) provided and/or the relevance of your reading.

6. Analysis/Synthesis Question: Why is this important?

Teachers begin each class asking the critical questions, and if the student cannot answer at the first two levels (the first two questions), then he or she is not allowed to test or progress further. The student is advised to study and review.

During the first week of using the critical questions, a bright young man explained to his teacher that he could no longer skim the assignment and find the answer. Our teachers all knew this student, and his statement validated the purpose of having the questions at the ready as a formative assessment tool.

Teachers chart the level of questions a student reaches each week, as this shows if the student can answer at a higher level of cognition. Charting every student daily has been a huge change for teachers. It took a semester to be fully implemented, as teachers continuously improved in asking and charting the student scores.

Our critical questions are not a silver bullet in improving student achievement, but they have become part of our daily routine in seeing that students are progressing toward higher levels of cognition, reading with a purpose, and using academic language to communicate with their teachers. The California High School Exit Examination (CAHSEE) data listed in Figure 7.1, showing the percentage of correct answers, justify our use of critical questions as part of student learning.

Additionally, the average score on the essay portion of CAHSEE has also improved over the past two years.

Our teachers are in the process of revising the critical questions for continued improvement.

FIGURE 7.1	Five Years of CAHSEE Results for the C.L.A.S.S. Program				
	2008	**2009**	**2010**	**2011**	**2012**
Writing Strategies	20%	34%	37%	45%	46%
Written Conventions	21%	49%	48%	51%	51%

CHAPTER 8

Now What?

As we have thought together about questions and the role of those questions in our classrooms, we hope that you have been encouraged to think, reflect, and learn ways to change your instructional practices. We started by recognizing that questions are terrific for:

- Helping people ponder, consider, and think deeply
- Reminding us that all brains are wired to learn
- Creating connections between people, because learning is a social experience

The whole purpose of our exploration has been the power of questions within the content areas to help student really "get it." As we bring our exploration to a close, we ask that you think about questions in three specific areas of your instructional practice:

- Planning
- Implementing
- Reflecting

Planning

1. Be intentional.

So much of what we do in the classroom is question-heavy. Teachers use questions so much that students may become desensitized to their importance. Sometimes we present many rhetorical questions—and those don't even require answers. Or we ask questions when we think that doing so softens a directive.

In *Beyond Monet,* Bennett and Rolheiser (2001) suggest that framing a question can be done best by a statement that leads to the question. They call it the focus statement. Before asking a question, the teacher already frames what will come next for the student response. For example, "Share with your partner please. What are endorphins? What are the connections between endorphins and laughter?" (p. 58). By using a focus statement first, there is more attention given to the question itself. Providing focus statements is just one way to be more intentional.

2. Be aware of "levels," for both age and cognition.

Sometimes teachers forget just what is age-appropriate. It happens both when we ask students to perform tasks beyond their developmental stages, and when we underestimate what is age-appropriate.

John Hattie (2009, 2012) points out that Piagetian teaching has an effect. Knowing that students at the primary grades are concrete thinkers opens the opportunity for us to ask questions that take them with us from concrete thinking to the abstract thinking that may be required in the critical thinking tasks we want them to do. Being age-appropriate in the classroom is not a new thought, but it may be a good time to have a conversation with others who teach at our same level and "check" on what we are doing in our classrooms.

Bloom's Taxonomy (1956) sure stands the test of time for guiding teachers to questions that involve higher levels of thinking. Our tip is that we "take students with us" in the classroom. We would like to suggest that students can do more complex thinking even at young ages if the questions are age- and level-appropriate. We really like the studies cited to describe four levels suggested in the second edition of *Classroom Instruction That Works* (Dean, Hubbell, Pitler, and Stone, 2012, p. 52) because they describe what it would look like to "take the students with us."

Questions:

    a. involve naming objects or concepts and increase vocabulary.

    b. focus on organizing and classifying vocabulary.

    c. require higher-order reasoning.

    d. move to the abstract level.

This progression really involves the best of modeling for the sake of thinking and learning.

3. Use what you already have.

We are all busy with the work we are already engaged in, and implementing yet another strategy might seem like a lot. However, there is no need to reinvent the wheel here. Textbooks and ancillary materials are *full* of questions! Some don't even need much tweaking. However, it is important to study these materials well in advance of conducting classroom discussion so that you select just the right questions for your students and for your purposes.

We also have each other. Collaboration is so powerful and beneficial, both for our students and for us. Form a professional learning community to explore powerful questioning even further. Work together to prepare good questions to ask in your lessons; each member could take a few questions from the textbook or other resources on hand and rewrite them if need be.

Implementing

The chapters in this book have been about implementing questioning strategies to help students engage, clarify, and deepen their understanding as they learn. One of the goals we suggest in this book is that students ask their own questions. Many gifted teachers we have known over the years have found ways to do this. Students can learn about Bloom's Taxonomy, Webb's Depth of Knowledge, or any other framework for the complexity of questions. Younger children can learn about "thin" or "thick" questions—those that are "thick" are the ones that are robust and hard to answer. Students of any age can learn about the five "Ws" and the "H" long known to journalists: who, what, when, where, why, and how. It's not hard to help students understand that the "why" and "how" questions are usually richer for discussion.

We encourage you to teach students about powerful questions and have them create and track the difficulty levels of their questions. Provide feedback and allow them to give you feedback, too. When teachers work in partnership with their students to improve the quality of questioning in the classroom, everyone benefits.

Engage by:

- Practicing wonder yourself. Our own sense of wonder and learning will still be a great motivator for our students.

- Asking questions that you don't have the answers for so that you explore together.

- Listening for the answers to the questions you ask. We demonstrate respect for thinking through our active listening. Students learn to listen by watching how we listen.

Clarify thinking by:

- Using strong follow-up questions. Most of us don't do all our thinking in our first answer. A follow-up question is a wonderful invitation to keep thinking.

- Being silent. We as teachers find this hard to do sometimes. Parker Palmer refers to this as "holding a question." This is such a respectful, empowering practice.

- Paraphrasing what a student just said. When we hear our words come back to us, we can determine if that is what we are really thinking.

Deepen understanding by:

- Setting a pace in class that allows for time to answer reflective questions.

- Balancing when to make answering an individual act and when to encourage community sharing.

- Encouraging written expression of students' thinking.

- Having students come up with a question of their own that reflects their continuing synthesis of content.

- Posing a question that requires the students to create a visual, digital, or structural response.

Check back through the book to see how others have implemented questioning strategies.

Reflecting

We believe that metacognitive work in the classroom is for both students and teachers. Fullan and Hargreaves in their book *Professional Capital* (2012) write about "reflecting in" and "reflecting on" (p. 98). We practice reflecting *on* after something has happened to learn from it. By doing this we get better at being able to reflect *in* the moment. What a great way to frame skills that all learners need! The more we give ourselves the opportunity to reflect through strong questions, the more we will value it enough to do it with our students as well.

YOUR REFLECTION

It seems like an appropriate close to this book to conclude with each of us engaging in a bit of reflection. To help us practice, we have created this exercise. Enjoy!

I used to think ... and now I think.... In his book of the same title, Richard Elmore (2011) got many of us to open up our thinking with this phrase as twenty different educators speak about their own thinking on school reform.

So where are you now with your thinking about how you want to use questions?

I used to think ...

Now I think ...

What action step do you wish to take?

Cognitive Levels

ᘐᘐᘐ

BLOOM'S TAXONOMY

Most educators are quite familiar with Bloom's *Taxonomy of Educational Objectives* (Bloom, 1956). For many, understanding the levels of thinking represented in this taxonomy was a cornerstone of required educational methods courses.

In recent years, as educators have become increasingly focused on the accurate assessment of student learning, the original taxonomy has been revisited and revised. Unlike the original, the revised framework is two-dimensional. In the newer model, the two dimensions are cognitive process and knowledge. These two components operate like X and Y axes: the cognitive level (evident from a verb that represents student learning) would be placed on the horizontal axis, and the type of knowledge (evident from the nouns that represent what the student is to learn) would be placed on the vertical.

The six cognitive processes in the revised taxonomy are *remember, understand, apply, analyze, evaluate,* and *create.* These are just slightly different from the original six levels of Bloom's Taxonomy. The four categories of knowledge in the revised taxonomy are factual, conceptual, procedural, and metacognitive.

This revised taxonomy works well with the "unwrapping" process and later, in designing effective assessment items. In order to place an objective in the taxonomy, teachers must first "unwrap" a standard to discover what it requires cognitively (the verb) and knowledge-wise (the nouns that delineate content and concepts). Once they have determined the correct placement, then the "bare bones" of the assessment items are set. However, the placement is important, because different types of objectives require different approaches to assessment (Anderson & Krathwohl, 2001, p. 8).

Thus, even though the list below contains only verbs that represent student learning, it is important to "unwrap" standards and ensure each standard is placed in the taxonomy table before designing appropriate assessment items.

Cognitive process 1: To *remember*

To remember is to retrieve relevant knowledge from long-term memory. (Anderson & Krathwohl, 2001, p. 67)

Verbs associated with this level: **tell, list, define, label, recite, recall, retrieve, name, record, relate, recognize, identify, describe, examine, group, locate, match, say, show, write.**

Cognitive process 2: To *understand*

To understand is to construct meaning from instructional messages, including oral, written, and graphic communication. (Anderson & Krathwohl, 2001, p. 67)

Verbs associated with this level: **interpret, clarify, paraphrase, represent, translate, exemplify, illustrate, classify, categorize, summarize, generalize, infer, conclude, predict, compare, contrast, match, explain, construct, differentiate, distinguish, reorganize.**

Cognitive process 3: To *apply*

To apply is to carry out or use a procedure in a given situation. (Anderson & Krathwohl, 2001, p. 67)

Verbs associated with this level: **apply, execute, carry out, implement, use, construct, model, display, illustrate.**

Cognitive process 4: To *analyze*

To analyze is to break material into its constituent parts and determine how the parts relate to one another and to an overall structure or purpose. (Anderson & Krathwohl, 2001, p. 68)

Verbs associated with this level: **differentiate, determine, discriminate, distinguish, focus, select, organize, integrate, outline, structure, deconstruct, solve (a problem), experiment, investigate, reduce, attribute, connect, ascertain.**

Cognitive process 5: To *evaluate*

To evaluate is to make judgments based on criteria and standards. (Anderson & Krathwohl, 2001, p. 68)

Verbs associated with this level: **check, coordinate, detect, monitor, test, judge, critique, appraise, criticize, defend, justify, assess, prioritize, award, convince, discriminate, order, rank, recommend, support.**

Cognitive process 6: To *create*

To create is to put elements together to form a coherent or functional whole; reorganize elements into a new pattern or structure; invent a product. (Anderson & Krathwohl, 2001, p. 68)

Verbs associated with this level: **make, generate, hypothesize, plan, design, produce, construct, compose, formulate, invent, develop, refine, transform, originate, test, execute.**

WEBB'S DEPTH OF KNOWLEDGE
FOR ELA, MATH, AND SCIENCE

The following charts, created by Karin Hess (2006), demonstrate the relationship between cognitive process systems.

English Language Arts/Social Studies Examples	Webb's Depth of Knowledge Levels			
Bloom's Taxonomy	Level 1 Recall & Reproduction	Level 2 Skills & Concepts	Level 3 Strategic Thinking/ Reasoning	Level 4 Extended Thinking
Knowledge Define, duplicate, label, list, memorize, name, order, recognize, relate, recall, reproduce, state	• List/generate ideas for writing or research • Recall, recognize, or locate basic facts, ideas, principles, concepts • Identify/describe key figures, places, or events in a particular context			
Comprehension Classify, describe, discuss, explain, express, identify, indicate, locate, recognize, report, restate, review, select, translate	• Write a simple sentence • Select appropriate word(s) to use in context when meaning is evident • Identify or describe characters, setting, plot, problem, solution • Describe or explain: who, what, where, when	• Determine or recognize main ideas/general-izations • Take and organize notes around common ideas/topics • Summarize ideas/events • Make basic inferences or logical predictions from text • Explain relationships/ cause-effect	• Write full composition using various sentence types and structures to meet purposes • Explain, generalize, or connect ideas using supporting evidence • Make inferences about theme or author's purpose	• Write full composition demonstrating synthesis and analysis of complex ideas • Compare multiple works by same author across time periods, genres, etc.

English Language Arts/Social Studies Examples	Webb's Depth of Knowledge Levels			
Bloom's Taxonomy	Level 1 Recall & Reproduction	Level 2 Skills & Concepts	Level 3 Strategic Thinking/ Reasoning	Level 4 Extended Thinking
Application Apply, choose, demonstrate, dramatize, employ, illustrate, interpret, practice, schedule, sketch, solve, use, write	• Apply spelling, grammar, punctuation, conventions, rules in writing • Use structures (pre/suffix) or relationships (synonym) to determine word meaning • Use resources to edit/revise	• Write paragraph using a basic structure or template • Edit final draft for mechanics and conventions • Use context clues to determine meaning • Use text features to find information	• Edit final draft for meaning/ progression of ideas • Apply a concept in other/new contexts • Support ideas with examples, citations, details, elaboration, quotations, text references	• Define and illustrate common social, historical, economic, or geographical themes and how they interrelate
Analysis Analyze, appraise, calculate, categorize, compare, criticize, discriminate, distinguish, examine, experiment	• Identify specific information contained in maps, charts, tables, graphs, or diagrams	• Analyze a paragraph for simple organizational structure • Determine fiction/ nonfiction; fact/opinion • Describe purpose of text features • Identify use of literary devices	• Analyze an essay • Compare information within or across text passages • Analyze interrelation- ships among text elements, situations, events, or ideas • Analyze use of literary devices	• Analyze multiple works by the same author across time periods, genres • Analyze complex/ abstract themes

English Language Arts/Social Studies Examples	Webb's Depth of Knowledge Levels			
Bloom's Taxonomy	Level 1 Recall & Reproduction	Level 2 Skills & Concepts	Level 3 Strategic Thinking/ Reasoning	Level 4 Extended Thinking
Synthesis Rearrange, assemble, collect, compose, create, design, develop, formulate, manage, organize, plan, propose, set up, write	• Brainstorm ideas, concepts, or perspectives related to a topic		• Synthesize information within one source or text • Develop a model for a complex situation	• Synthesize information across multiple sources or texts • Given a situation/ problem, research, define, and describe the situation/ problem and provide alternate solutions
Evaluation Appraise, argue, assess, choose, compare, defend, estimate, judge, predict, rate, select, support, value			• Cite evidence and develop logical argu-ment for concepts • Make and support generalizations using text evidence	• Gather, analyze, and evaluate information to draw conclusions • Evaluate relevancy, accuracy, completeness of information from multiple sources

Source: Hess, 2006

Math Examples	Webb's Depth of Knowledge Levels			
Bloom's Taxonomy	Level 1 Recall & Reproduction	Level 2 Skills & Concepts	Level 3 Strategic Thinking/ Reasoning	Level 4 Extended Thinking
Knowledge Define, duplicate, label, list, memorize, name, order, recognize, relate, recall, reproduce, state	• Recall, recognize, or locate basic facts, ideas, principles • Recall or identify conversions between and among representations or numbers, or within and between customary and metric measures			
Comprehension Classify, describe, discuss, explain, express, identify, indicate, locate, recognize, report, restate, review, select, translate	• Make conversions between and among representations or numbers, or within and between customary and metric measures • Evaluate an expression • Locate points on a grid or number line • Solve a one-step problem	• Specify and explain relationships (cause/effect; how or why; nonexamples/ examples) • Make and record observations • Take notes to organize information/ ideas • Summarize results or concepts • Make basic inferences or logical predictions from data/ observations	• Use concepts to solve nonroutine problems • Explain, generalize, or connect ideas using supporting evidence • Make or justify conjectures • Explain thinking when more than one response is possible • Explain phenomena in terms of concepts	• Relate mathematical or scientific concepts to other content areas or concepts • Develop generalizations of the results obtained and the strategies used and apply them to new problem situations

Math Examples	Webb's Depth of Knowledge Levels			
Bloom's Taxonomy	Level 1 Recall & Reproduction	Level 2 Skills & Concepts	Level 3 Strategic Thinking/ Reasoning	Level 4 Extended Thinking
Application Apply, choose, demonstrate, dramatize, employ, illustrate, interpret, practice, schedule, sketch, solve, use, write	• Follow simple procedures (recipe-type directions) • Calculate, measure, apply a rule • Apply an algorithm or formula (area, perimeter, etc.) • Represent in words or diagrams a scientific concept or relationship	• Select a procedure according to criteria and perform it • Solve routine problem applying multiple concepts or decision points • Retrieve information from a table, graph, or figure, and use it to solve a problem requiring multiple steps	• Design investigation for a specific purpose or research question • Conduct a designed investigation • Use concepts to solve nonroutine problems • Use reasoning, planning, and evidence	• Select or devise approach among many alternatives to solve a problem • Conduct a project that specifies a problem, identifies solution paths, solves the problem, and reports results
Analysis Analyze, appraise, calculate, categorize, compare, criticize, discriminate, distinguish, examine, experiment	• Retrieve information from a table or graph	• Categorize, classify materials based on characteristics • Compare/ contrast figures or data • Select appropriate graph and display data • Interpret data from a simple graph • Extend a pattern	• Compare information within or across data sets or texts • Analyze and draw conclusions from data • Generalize a pattern • Interpret data from complex graph	• Analyze multiple sources of evidence • Analyze complex/ abstract themes • Gather, analyze, and evaluate information

Math Examples	Webb's Depth of Knowledge Levels			
Bloom's Taxonomy	Level 1 Recall & Reproduction	Level 2 Skills & Concepts	Level 3 Strategic Thinking/ Reasoning	Level 4 Extended Thinking
Synthesis Rearrange, assemble, collect, compose, create, design, develop, formulate, manage, organize, plan, propose, set up, write	• Brainstorm ideas, concepts, or perspectives related to a topic	• Use models to represent mathematical concepts	• Synthesize information within one source or text • Formulate an original problem given a situation • Develop a scientific/ mathematical model for a complex situation	• Synthesize information across multiple sources or texts • Design a mathematical model to inform and solve a practical or abstract situation
Evaluation Appraise, argue, assess, choose, compare, defend, estimate, judge, predict, rate, select, support, value			• Cite evidence and develop logical argument for concepts • Describe, compare and contrast solution methods • Verify reasonableness of results	• Gather, analyze, and evaluate information to draw conclusions • Apply understanding in a novel way, provide argument or justification for the application

Source: Hess, 2006

Portfolio Guidelines and Rubric for Ms. Market's Consumer Living Class

⤳⤲

PORTFOLIO PROJECT

For each of the areas below, you must include an artifact to show your knowledge in that area and a reflection to show your growth. The artifacts and reflections will be uploaded to a portfolio Web site. This assignment will be ongoing throughout the semester. There are due dates throughout the semester to keep you on task.

- Define artifact:
  - Give examples:
- Define reflection:
  - Why is this so important?
  - Questions to ask while reflecting:
    - What went well?
    - What didn't?
    - What would you change for next time?
    - How would this work in your own classroom some day?

Areas of Portfolio
- Observations of elementary students
  - Anecdotal
  - Checklist
  - Rating Scales

- Classroom Environment
  - Creating an environment of respect and rapport
  - Establishing culture for learning
  - Managing classroom procedures
  - Managing student behavior
  - Organizing physical space
- Instruction
  - Communicating with students clearly and accurately
  - Assessment
- Planning and Preparation
  - 3 lesson plans
- Resume
  - Must be applicable to use for a job working with children
- Observations from instructor(s)
  - 2–3 observations will be done by the elementary instructor or your elementary mentoring instructor

Portfolio Checklist

Area		✔ Completed	Artifact Idea	Reflection
Observations				
Due: 11/28	Anecdotal Observation			
Due: 11/28	Checklist Observation			
Due: 11/28	Rating Scale Observation			
Classroom Management				
Due: 12/5	Creating an environment of respect and rapport			
Due: 12/12	Managing classroom procedures			
Due: 12/12	Managing student behavior			
Due: 12/19	Organizing physical space			

Area		✔ Completed	Artifact Idea	Reflection
Instruction				
Due: 12/19	Communi-cating clearly and accurately			
Due: 1/6	Assessment			
Planning and Preparation				
Due: 1/6	Lesson Plan #1 or Lucy Laney Reflection		2 Paragraph Reflection	
Due: 1/13	Lesson Plan #2—random		Lesson Plan	Peer Review
Due: 1/13	Lesson Plan #3—does not need to be uploaded		Final Lesson Plan	Reflection

Creating a Web Site Using Google

- Go to google.com
- Sign in. (You will need to create an account if you do not have one. If you create an account, it will ask for your current email address. You will need to verify the new account via your current account. Once it has been verified, sign in.)

Once you are signed in, you will click on "sites" at the top of your Web page. If you do not see "sites," click "more" and scroll down to "sites."

- Once you are in "sites," click "create."
- You may pick any template you'd like.
- Click "create" at the top to begin your page.

Changing Privacy Settings

- Click "Change" next to the phrase "Public to anyone."
- Change it to anyone who has the link.
- Add your teacher's email address to share the link.

Editing Your Page

- At the top right of the screen, you will see a pencil and a page button.
- Click the pencil button to edit your page. This tool will allow you to make columns in the layout and add images, videos, etc.
- **SAVE OFTEN!!!**

The page button will be used to add a page. You will need to name your page and then you will see it on the left side navigating bar.

Rubric

This rubric should be completed by the elementary teacher while the high school student teaches. Please share any comments, critiques, or praise.

	4	3	2	1
PREPARATION	Well prepared, punctual, professional, has clear understanding of lesson	Prepared, mostly professional, refers back to lesson during teaching	Somewhat prepared, unprofessional at times, refers back to lesson during teaching	Unprepared, unprofessional, often refers back to lesson during teaching
ENGAGEMENT	Responsive to children and their needs, adapts when needed, gives praise, smiles	Somewhat responsive to children and their needs, makes few adaptations, gives praise, smiles	Not responsive to children and their needs, makes few adaptations, gives few smiles and/or praises	Not responsive to children and their needs, makes no adaptations, gives few smiles and/or praises
COMMUNICATION	Confident and clear voice, age appropriate, directions are clear, positive, appropriate volume	Somewhat confident and clear voice, age appropriate, directions are mostly clear, positive, appropriate volume	Unconfident and shaky voice, age appropriate, directions are not often clear, positive, appropriate volume	Unconfident and shaky voice, age appropriate, directions are not often clear, not always positive, inappropriate volume

	4	3	2	1
CLASSROOM MANAGEMENT	High school student has control of the classroom, elementary students are focused and on task, transitions are used when needed, and techniques are used to get students back on track	High school student mostly has control of the classroom, elementary students are focused and on task, transitions are sometimes used when needed, and techniques are used to get students back on track	High school student does not have control of the classroom, elementary students are sometimes focused and on task, transitions are sometimes used when needed, and techniques are used to get students back on track	High school student does not have control of the classroom, elementary students are sometimes focused and on task, transitions are not used when needed, and techniques are not used to get students back on track
LESSON OBJECTIVES	The lesson objectives are clearly stated and meet the elementary teacher's request for the lesson. The lesson helps elementary students reach this objective.	The lesson objectives are stated and mostly meet the elementary teacher's request for the lesson. The lesson will help elementary students reach this objective.	The lesson objectives are stated and slightly meet the elementary teacher's request for the lesson. The lesson will not help the majority of elementary students reach this objective.	The lesson objectives are stated and do not meet the elementary teacher's request for the lesson. The lesson will not help the majority of elementary students reach this objective.

Mr. Lee's Schoology Video Discussion

REAL-TIME VIDEO DISCUSSION

This is an activity that requires each student to have access to a discussion board. It is very straightforward for most students. As students watch the video as a class, they should make comments or ask questions as they come to mind. The teacher can choose to pause the video as needed to allow time for students to complete their thoughts. Every time they post, the thread refreshes. They can see if someone has responded to their post and thus reply. This all happens very quickly, so the instructor must hit F5 or click refresh frequently to monitor the discussion.

The following is a view of what the activity would look like in Schoology.

Phase 1: Watch video and pick out interesting points.

GMO (Genetically Modified Food)

Created by CALEB LEE on Today at 12:14 pm

First reactions DURING the Video about GMO. Make a comment that expresses and intellectual concern. NO JOKES.

Phase 1: Real time comments, Feel free to respond to each other as well.

After Video: Go to Next Discussion Thread GMO Investigates

TEDxAustin Robyn O'Brien 2011 – YouTube
Robyn shares her personal story and how it inspired her current path as a "Real Food" evangelist. Grounded in a successful Wall Street career that was more i...

Snapshots of student discussion: This is the kind of dialogue we should be looking for from our students regarding content.

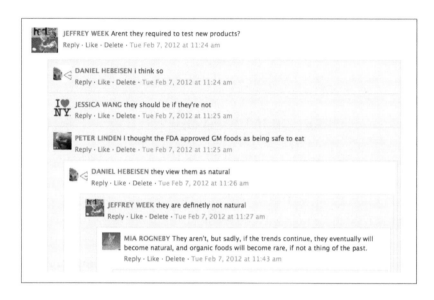

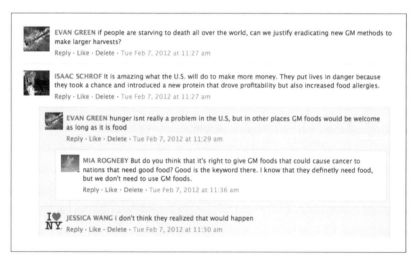

Phase 2: Research and continue discussion.

GMO Investigation

Created by CALEB LEE on Tue Feb 7, 2012 at 11:42 am

Phase 2: Invesigation (A–L Refute) (L–Z Confirm)

Find a reliable source that can benefit your case for or against.

Post a very short quote include the web address of the source.

Add your own explaination about the data you found.

Below: 1st link supports video
2nd link has info against video claims(sort through)

 GMO news and articles

 Search Results: safe genetically ...

Student research discussion would include active links to research. Students should be asked to click on others' research links and verify.

REFERENCES

Achieve, Inc. (2007). *Closing the expectations gap 2007: An annual 50-state progress report on the alignment of high school policies with the demands of college and work.* Washington, DC: Author. Retrieved from http://www.achieve.org/files/50-state-07-Final.pdf

ACT. (2006). *Reading between the lines: What the ACT reveals about college readiness in reading.* Retrieved from http://www.act.org/research/ policymakers/reports/reading.html

Ainsworth, L. (2003). *Unwrapping the standards.* Englewood, CO: Lead + Learn Press.

Alliance for Excellent Education. (2011, April). *Engineering solutions to the national crisis in literacy: How to make good on the promise of the Common Core State Standards.* Retrieved from http://www.all4ed.org/ publication_material/PolicyBrief/EngineeringSolutionsLiteracy

Anderson, L. W., & Krathwohl, D. R. (2001). *A taxonomy for learning, teaching, and assessing: A revision of Bloom's taxonomy of education objectives.* New York: Longman.

Anderson, N. J. (2002, April). *The role of metacognition in second language teaching and learning.* Retrieved from http://www.cal.org/resources/ digest/0110anderson.html

Bennett, A., & Rolheiser, C. (2001). *Beyond Monet: The artful science of instructional integration.* Toronto, ON: Bookation.

Black, P., & Wiliam, D. (1998). *Inside the black box: Raising standards through classroom assessment.* London: School of Education, King's College.

Bloom, B. S. (1956). *Taxonomy of educational objectives: The classification of educational goals, handbook 1: The cognitive domain.* New York: Longman.

Bridgeland, J. M., Dilulio, J. J., & Morison, K. B. (2006). *The silent epidemic: Perspectives of high school dropouts.* A report by Civic Enterprises in association with Peter D. Hart Research Associates for the Bill & Melinda Gates Foundation. Retrieved from http://www.ignitelearning .com/pdf/TheSilentEpidemic3-06FINAL.pdf

Clarke, S. (2001). *Unlocking formative assessment.* London: Hodder Education.

Clarke, S. (2005). *Formative assessment in action.* London: Hodder Murray.

Clarke, S. (2008). *Active learning through formative assessment.* London: Hodder Education.

Copeland, M. (2005.) *Socratic circles: Fostering critical and creative thinking in middle and high school.* Portland, ME: Stenhouse.

Danielson, C. (2007). *Enhancing professional practice: A framework for teaching.* (2nd ed.). Alexandria, VA: ASCD.

Davies, A. (2012). *Slowing down to the speed of learning.* Presented at the Fourth Annual Assessment and Leadership Institute, Minnetonka, Minnesota, June 27–28.

Dean, C. B., Hubbell, E. R., Pitler, H., & Stone, B. (2012). *Classroom instruction that works.* (2nd ed.). Alexandria, VA: ASCD.

Driscoll, M. (1999). *Fostering algebraic thinking: A guide for teachers, grades 6–10.* Portsmouth, NH: Heinemann.

DuFour, R., & Eaker, R. (1998). *Professional learning communities at work.* Bloomington, IN: Solution Tree.

Dweck, C. (2006). *Mindset: The new psychology of success.* New York: Ballantine.

Elmore, R. (Ed.). (2011). *I used to think . . . and now I think . . .: Twenty leading educators reflect on the work on school reform.* Cambridge, MA: Harvard Education Press.

Erickson, S., Anderson, D., Hillen, J., & Wiebe, A. (2003). *Proportional reasoning.* Fresno, CA: AIMS Education Foundation.

Fisher, D., & Frey, N. (2008). *Word wise and content rich.* Portsmouth, NH: Heinemann.

Frey, N., & Fisher, D. (2010, October). Identifying instructional moves during guided learning. *The Reading Teacher, 64*(2), 84–95.

Fullan, M. (2008). *What's worth fighting for in the principalship?* New York: Teacher's College Press.

Fullan, M., & Hargreaves, A. (2012). *Professional capital: Transforming teaching in every school.* New York: Teacher's College, Columbia University.

Gallagher, K. (n.d.). *Assessment that improves student writing.* Retrieved from http://www.cedu.niu.edu/oep/conferences/LiteracyConference/handouts/gallagher/Assessment2.pdf

Gibbs, J. (1987). *Tribes: A process for social development and cooperative learning.* Cloverdale, CA: CenterSource Systems.

Goodlad, J. (1984). *A place called school.* New York: McGraw Hill.

Graham, S., & Perin, D. (2007). *Writing next: Effective strategies to improve writing of adolescents in middle and high schools—A report to Carnegie Corporation of New York.* Washington, DC: Alliance for Excellent Education.

Graves, D. (1982). Six guideposts to a successful writing conference. *Learning, 11*(4), 76–77.

Hattie, J. (2009). *Visible learning: A synthesis of over 800 meta-analyses relating to achievement.* New York: Routledge.

Hattie, J. (2012). *Visible learning for teachers.* New York: Routledge.

Heller, R., & Greenleaf, C. (2007, June). *Literacy instruction in the content areas: Getting to the core of middle and high school improvement.* Washington, DC: Alliance for Excellent Education.

Hess, K. K. (2006). *Cognitive complexity: Applying Webb DOK levels to Bloom's taxonomy.* Dover, NH: National Center for Assessment.

Hillocks, G. (2010, July). Teaching argument for critical thinking and writing: An introduction. *English Journal, 99*(6), 24–32.

Himmele, P., & Himmele, W. (2011). *Total participation techniques: Making every student an active learner.* Alexandria, VA: ASCD.

Lambert, C. (2012, March/April). Twilight of the lecture. *Harvard Magazine, 114*(4), 23–27. Retrieved from http://harvardmagazine.com/2012/03/twilight-of-the-lecture

Leeds, D. (2000). *The 7 powers of questions: Secrets to successful communication in life and at work.* New York: Berkley Publishing Group.

Lemov, D. (2010). *Teach like a champion: 49 techniques that put students on the path to college.* San Francisco, CA: Jossey-Bass.

Leven, T., & Long, R. (1981). *Effective instruction.* Washington, DC: Association for Supervision and Curriculum Development.

Llewellyn, D. (2004). *Inquire within: Implementing inquiry-based science standards.* Thousand Oaks, CA: Corwin.

Marzano, R. (2007). *The art and science of teaching: A comprehensive framework for effective instruction.* Alexandria, VA: ASCD.

Marzano, R. (2010, April). Teaching inference. *Educational Leadership, 67*(7), 80–81.

Marzano, R., & Heflebower, T. (2012). *Teaching & assessing 21st century skills.* Bloomington, IN: Marzano Research Laboratory.

Marzano, R., & Kendall, J. S. (2007). *The new taxonomy of educational objectives.* Thousand Oaks, CA: Sage.

Marzano, R., Pickering, D., & Pollock, J. (2001). *Classroom instruction that works.* Alexandria, VA: ASCD.

McCain, T. (2005). *Teaching for tomorrow.* Thousand Oaks, CA: Corwin.

National Center for Education Statistics (NCES). (2006). *Progress in international reading literacy study (PIRLS).* Retrieved from http://nces.ed.gov/surveys/pirls/

National Center for Education Statistics (NCES). (2012). *National Assessment of Educational Progress.* Retrieved from http://nces.ed .gov/nationsreportcard/

National Commission on Writing. (2004). *Writing: A ticket to work . . . or a ticket out: A survey of business leaders.* Retrieved from http://www.collegeboard.com/prod_downloads/writingcom/writing-ticket-to-work.pdf

National Committee on Science Education Standards and Assessment; National Research Council. (1996). *National science education standards.* Author.

National Council for the Social Studies. (1992). *National curriculum standards for social studies: Executive summary.* Retrieved from http://www.socialstudies.org/standards/execsummary

National Governors Association Center for Best Practices and Council of Chief State School Officers. (2010). *Common core state standards.* Washington, DC: Author.

National Science Teachers Association. (2004). *NSTA position statement: Scientific inquiry.* Retrieved from http://www.nsta.org/about/ positions/inquiry.aspx

National Science Teachers Association. (2007). *Position statement: The integral role of laboratory investigations in science instruction.* Retrieved from http://www.nsta.org/about/positions/laboratory.aspx

Norton-Meier, L., Hand, B., Hockenberry, L., & Wise, K. (2008). *Questions, claims, and evidence: The important place of argument in children's science writing.* Portsmouth, NH: Heinemann.

Nuthall, G. (2007). *The hidden lives of learners.* Wellington, NZ: New Zealand Council for Educational Research.

Organisation for Economic Co-operation and Development (OECD). (2006). *Education at a glance 2006: Briefing note for the United States.* Paris: Author.

Palmer, P. (1993). *To know as we are known.* New York: HarperCollins Publishers.

Palmer, P. (1997). *The courage to teach.* San Francisco, CA: Jossey-Bass.

Peery, A. (2009). *Power strategies for effective teaching.* Englewood, CO: The Leadership and Learning Center.

Peressini, D., Borko, H., Romagnano, L., Knuth, E., & Willis, C. (2004). A conceptual framework for learning to teach secondary mathematics: A situative perspective. *Educational Studies in Mathematics, 56*(1), 67–96.

Peterson, D., & Taylor, B. (2012, February). Using higher order questioning to accelerate students' growth in reading. *The Reading Teacher, 65*(5), 295–304.

Pianta, R. C., Belsky, J., Houts, R., & Morrison, F. (2007, March). Teaching: Opportunities to learn in America's elementary classrooms. *Science, 315*(5820), 1795–1796. Retrieved from http://www.sciencemag.org/cgi/content/full/315/5820/1795

Pollock, J. (2007). *Improving student learning one teacher at a time.* Alexandria, VA: ASCD.

Powell, A., Farrar, E., & Cohen, D. (1986). *The shopping mall high school: Winners and losers in the educational marketplace.* New York: Houghton Mifflin.

Reeves, D. B. (2010). Available at http://www.aasa.org/uploadedFiles/Resources/files/Feb2011-BLMIH1%20Flyer-110127.pdf

Ritchhart, R., Church, M., & Morrison, K. (2011). *Making thinking visible: How to promote engagement, understanding, and independence for all learners.* San Francisco, CA: Jossey-Bass.

Robinson, K. (2010). *Changing education paradigms.* RSA Animate. Retrieved from http://www.youtube.com/watch?v=zDZFcDGpL4U

Rose, M. (2005). *Lives on the boundary: A moving account of the struggles and achievements of America's educationally underprepared.* New York: Penguin.

Rosenthal, R., & Jacobson, L. (1966). Teachers' expectancies: Determinants of pupils' IQ gains. *Psychological Reports, 19,* 115–118.

Rothstein, D., & Santana, L. (2011). *Make just one change: Teach students to ask their own questions.* Cambridge, MA: Harvard Education Press.

Rowe, M. B. (1986, January). Wait time: Slowing down may be a way of speeding up. *Journal of Teacher Education, 37*(1), 43–50.

Schell, E., & Fisher, D. (2007). *Teaching social studies: A literacy-based approach.* Upper Saddle River, NJ: Pearson Education.

Schmoker, M. (2001, October 24). The Crayola curriculum. *Education Week, 21*(8), 42–44.

Schmoker, M. (2006). *Results now: How we can achieve unprecedented improvements in teaching and learning.* Alexandria, VA: ASCD.

Schmoker, M. (2009, October). *The opportunity: From brutal facts to the best school we've ever had.* Placer County Office of Education.

Schmoker, M. (2011). *Focus: Elevating the essentials to radically improve student learning.* Alexandria, VA: ASCD.

Schmoker, M., & Graff, G. (2011, April 20). More argument, fewer standards. *Education Week, 30*(28), 31–33.

Sizer, T. (1992). *Horace's compromise: The dilemma of the American high school.* New York: Houghton Mifflin.

Stein, E. (2011, June). Teaching secrets: Asking the right questions. *Education Week.* Available online at http://www.edweek.org/tm/articles/2011/ 05/31/effectivequestioning.html

Sullivan, P., & Lilburn, P. (2002). *Good questions for math teaching: Why ask them and what to ask.* Sausalito, CA: Math Solutions Publications.

Tolan, M. (2012, August). Personal communication.

Voigt, J. (1995). Thematic patterns of interaction and sociomathematical norms. In P. Cobb & H. Bauersfeld (Eds.), *The Emergence of Mathematical Meaning,* (pp. 163–201). Hillsdale, NJ: Lawrence Erlbaum Associates.

Vygotsky, L. S. (1978). *Mind and society: The development of higher mental processes.* Cambridge, MA: Harvard University Press.

Walsh, J. A., & Sattes, B. D. (2005). *Quality questioning: Research-based practice to engage every learner.* Thousand Oaks, CA: Sage.

Wieners, B. (2011). Lego is for girls. *Bloomberg Businessweek.* Retrieved from http://www.businessweek.com/magazine/lego-is-for-girls -12142011.html#p1

Wiggins, G., & McTighe, J. (2001). *Understanding by design.* Alexandria, VA: ASCD.

Wiggins, G., & McTighe, J. (2005). *Understanding by design* .(2nd ed.). Alexandria, VA: ASCD.

Wiggins, G., & McTighe, J. (2006). Summer Conference on Differentiating Instruction and Understanding by Design: Powerful Keys to Student Learning. Denver, CO.

Wiliam, D. (2011). *Embedded formative assessment.* Bloomington, IN: Solution Tree.

Willingham, D. T. (2009). *Why don't students like school? A cognitive scientist answers questions about how the mind works and what it means for the classroom.* San Francisco, CA: Jossey-Bass.

Willis, J. (2008). *How your child learns best: Brain-friendly strategies you can use to ignite your child's learning and increase school success.* Naperville, IL: Sourcebooks.

INDEX